THE
$\mathcal{G}$LASS $\mathcal{E}$LEVATOR

The Glass Elevator:
A Guide to Leadership Presence for Women on the Rise

Copyright © 2012 Ora Shtull

Published by

85Broads

An Exclusive Global Women's Network
115 E. Putnam Avenue, Courtyard Level
Greenwich, CT 06830
www.85broads.com

ISBN 13:978-0-9850579-0-9

Printed in the United States of America

To order copies of this book for special groups or programs, please visit
www.oracoaching.com.

Editing and book design by Stacey Aaronson
www.creative-collaborations.com

THE GLASS ELEVATOR

A GUIDE TO
LEADERSHIP PRESENCE
FOR WOMEN
ON THE RISE

ORA SHTULL

85Broads

For Noa, Carmel, and other young women who will ride the glass elevator to the top.

And for Tai and other young men who will ride along with them in equal partnership.

$\mathscr{T}$ABLE OF $\mathscr{C}$ONTENTS

$\mathcal{I}$NTRODUCTION

FROM GLASS SLIPPERS TO GLASS CEILINGS, women have spent many hours debating whether their success is limited by or dependent on others. The truth is life is never perfectly fair, but your success – professionally and personally – is essentially up to you.

Yes, I've heard the bad news that only 2.5% of corporate America's CEOs are women. I've seen the studies that women on average make 75% of what men make. We all know the ubiquitous term "the glass ceiling" (according to longstanding perception, an invisible limit in corporations that women find difficult, if not impossible, to surmount). We've all imagined the oft-quoted act of breaking through the glass ceiling – or at minimum, putting a sizable crack in it.

That analogy strikes me as both funny and impractical. Who goes through a ceiling? Why bother putting a crack in it? Cracking glass sounds a bit risky to me. When I think about glass ceilings, I hear shattering and picture sharp projectiles rushing in my direction. No, thank you. In fact, why even consider going through a ceiling? Isn't there an easier way to get upstairs?

You bet there is. If you have your sights set on a C-level position in your company (any position that starts with a C, like CEO), you don't have to crack your head on a ceiling, glass or otherwise, to reach it.

There are safer routes, and there are skills you can master for your journey. They are transparent, not mysterious. That's why I urge you to sidestep the glass shards and consider the book you have in your hand a glass *elevator*, just waiting to take you to an office upstairs.

We women are holding down a multitude of positions in our own industries, with responsibilities as varied as the day is long. Each of us has her own unique goals. The idea of the "office upstairs" means something different to every one of us. It might be literal: an upper management position in your firm. Or it might be the idea of owning your own business. On the other hand, the office upstairs might represent where you want to be at some future point in your life. Ask yourself:

What does the "office upstairs" mean to me?

Take a moment. This question deserves your attention. Wherever the question leads you and however you personally define your "office," seeking it out invariably means that you will be more valuable and more valued.

A QUICK DETOUR: I am third-generation American. Unlike many of my friends who grew up surrounded by matronly grandmothers with strong European accents who could always be found cooking or feeding, my Grandma Flora, born in Brooklyn at the turn of the century, was petite, cute, and outrageously funny – and I can't remember one thing she ever cooked.

Flora was a strong personality and the belle of many a ball. In the twenties, she was a full-fledged flapper. She danced at speakeasies to the sound of jazz and smoked like a fiend. She hitchhiked to Washington D.C. with her girlfriends; I have the fun-filled photos. She was also strong-minded. When news surfaced that smoking was unhealthy, she quit cold turkey. No patches, pills, or behavioral therapy.

And Flora worked. She was a statistical stenographer. Before computers, people did spreadsheets manually. My grandmother worked at a bank, typing these spreadsheets on oversized typewriters. She was faster than the younger girls and she was perfectly accurate; she had to be – white-out had yet to be invented. And while her Brooklyn neighbors were working in groceries, Flora was proud to work in a "fancy" office. She was valued at the bank and, knowing her big personality, was likely the center of attention. She also made more money than her husband, Grandpa Nat, who worked first as a cloth-cutter in a factory and later as a gas station attendant.

Grandma Flora's daughter – my mother Rita – with four children and no modern-day nanny, also always worked. She chose a traditional field for women in her day: education. She began her career as a language teacher, then became a broader educator, a principal, and eventually earned the titles of Supervisor and Administrator. She too made more money than her husband, my father, who was a clergyman.

While each generation is presented with its own expectations and opportunities, neither Flora nor Rita felt that she was necessarily held back by her gender. Each focused on growth, learning, and excellence, pursuing the things that gave her satisfaction. It wasn't alchemy or luck that brought them to their goals, but rather the same skills that successful women are using today. I feel blessed by my legacy and my environment. Unlike many women in the world, I've never experienced barriers – or "ceilings" – to professional growth.

In today's world, women have growing aspirations in increasingly supportive environments. What I know in our cultural sphere is that we are all looking for jobs that allow us to achieve greater satisfaction in our lives – jobs that allow us to feel connected and where we can make a difference. What we all have in common is that we don't want to stagnate. We have no desire to be in the same positions our whole lives or earn the same salaries. What we want is to show our value and be compensated for it as we continue to grow professionally, always moving in an upward direction.

There is plenty of good news about women:

- For the first time, women have surpassed men in gaining bachelors degrees as well as advanced college degrees. These educational gains are leading to greater access to a wider range of jobs.
- Women make up more than half of the U.S. workforce, and the number is growing.
- More than half of the nation's wealth is now in the hands of women.
- Women make 80% of the buying decisions in this country.
- Women consistently outlive their male partners.
- Women-owned businesses are a growing, unstoppable force in the U.S. and world economies.
- Women are increasingly the primary breadwinners in their families.

With this backdrop of good news, ambitious women must power up their Leadership Presence to get where they want to go.

COACHING MEN AND WOMEN in New York's leading companies for nearly two decades, I have observed a direct correlation between certain executive behaviors and professional success. In the course of my practice, I have also noted leadership behaviors that differentiate men and women in the workplace. With that in mind, I developed tools and techniques tailored particularly to the needs of women striving for leadership growth.

My approach is based on my proprietary methodology – the Leadership Presence Coaching Model – which enhances a woman's ability to engage, connect, and influence in the workplace. In the coming pages, I will take you through the Leadership Presence skills you need to reach your goals and advance to your own desired "office upstairs." I will share tangible action steps to get you started and practical tools you will use every day.

Engage. Connect. Influence. These are the three essential components of Leadership Presence, each involving three skills (I think in threes).

Thus, each chapter in the book highlights one of the following nine skills you will need to be an effective leader.

Chapters 1, 2, and 3 include the three essential skills of *Engage*:

- ▲ Communicate with Oomph
- ▲ Strut Your Stuff
- ▲ Listen Like a Leader

Chapters 4, 5, and 6 include the three essential skills of *Connect*:

- ▲ Buddy Up with Your Boss
- ▲ Tango with Your Team
- ▲ Grow Your Tribe

Chapters 7, 8, and 9 include the three essential skills of *Influence*:

- ▲ Increase Your Influence
- ▲ Find the Me in Team
- ▲ Be Happy

Along with these nine Leadership Presence skills, every aspiring professional has three additional qualities that lend to success: self-awareness, not being afraid to sweat, and willingness to ask for support.

Self-awareness is your ability to recognize your strengths and limitations. It gives you insight into what drives you, what emotions affect you both positively and negatively, how you impact others, and ultimately, is the key to growth. It is no secret that the most potent and influential professionals are also the most self-aware. The more self-aware you are, the better you are at monitoring and regulating yourself, and the more confident and comfortable you are with yourself and with others.

Everyone knows the unfortunate someone with extraordinary skills who is promoted to a seemingly well-deserved position and then fails. It may have even been you. There is a lesson to be learned from these situations: skills, vision, and intellect are all good, but they're not enough. Effective leaders certainly must have the skills to match the position they are in, but they also must have self-awareness.

To that end, at the beginning of each chapter, you will find **The Ground Floor Quiz**. As simple and straightforward as this quiz is, its purpose is to trigger the process of gaining self-awareness – to help identify your strengths and to target your opportunities for growth.

Next is the capacity to **sweat**. No one ever procrastinated her way to the top – there is a direct correlation between success and hard work! We all know this, even if we sometimes wish otherwise.

Two of my long-term dreams were to compete in bodybuilding championships and to run marathons (OK, I know I'm an odd fish). The first thing I realized, of course, was that you don't just wake up one day and say, "Today I'm going to run a marathon and tomorrow I'm going to compete in a bodybuilding competition." You're not. In fact, the long and incredibly rewarding hours that I put in on the road and in the gym taught me that you have to break a sweat. And, if you're like me, you come to find out that those sweaty workouts can be as uplifting as winning the medals and taking home the trophies. Similarly, you don't wake up and say, "Today I will become an influential leader who makes a difference and has a robust salary." It takes action and hard work. It requires tripping and falling every once in a while and picking yourself back up. It takes time. It takes baby steps. It also entails breaking a sweat.

To aid you in this endeavor, at the end of every chapter I provide a section called **The Elevator Workout**. This is where I ask you to stop and be reflective for a moment. The Workout allows you to think back over the material we've just covered and see what resonated with you and what you truly found relevant. It also gives you an opportunity to put down on paper exactly what you'd like to work on and what you're willing to be held accountable for. The Elevator Workouts won't overwhelm you. In fact, this is where the baby steps come in. This is the time to choose one small thing to experiment with in the workplace and see how it works for you. Then, at the end, when you add up all the baby steps, you'll find yourself walking. The walking will lead to running. And a commitment to running may even lead to marathoning. Before you know it, you're exactly where you want to be.

Finally, strong professionals welcome **support.** There's an interesting piece of research worth sharing here: Women who seek out appropriate training and coaching are far more apt to increase their leadership effectiveness, to be given more responsibility, and to earn the trust of their peers and their boss ... oh, yes, and to increase their income. I have seen this many times from the amazing women I've coached and from the executives you will see profiled throughout this book. I've witnessed it firsthand inside some of the most progressive corporations in the country, where I've been honored to work with many of their most promising professionals.

The good news is that you don't need a formal executive coaching engagement to grow. Research shows that we can also benefit from informal coaching and support. That is why I wrote this book. For those of you without a company-sponsored executive coach, *The Glass Elevator* offers encouragement toward growth and success as well as a suite of unique and easily applicable tools to support you. So, start packing up your desk. You're moving up, and the journey begins now.

And, yes, while it may be true that women currently make up only a small percentage of CEOs across America, companies and organizations in every industry and field are benefiting from continually growing numbers of women in executive positions. One thing that the research has concluded beyond doubt is that diversity at the top – in particular with respect to color and gender – translates into higher returns in every industry. Even more telling is the fact that companies with the highest representation of women in top management experience better financial performance than companies with the lowest representation.

What does this mean? It's a heartening indication that companies in all industries are listening. But you and I both know that no one ever hands you power. You have to switch on that inner light so you'll be ready for the promise and the opportunity that await you.

So power up. (Someone hold the doors!) The glass elevator is waiting.

PART ONE
ENGAGE

THE GROUND FLOOR QUIZ
COMMUNICATE WITH OOMPH

I think about what I can contribute before I attend a meeting.

____Never   ____Sometimes   ____Always

I speak easily at meetings, without waiting to be called on.

____Never   ____Sometimes   ____Always

When I don't agree with an idea, I speak up.

____Never   ____Sometimes   ____Always

I use examples or anecdotes to back up or highlight my points.

____Never   ____Sometimes   ____Always

I talk about my work in terms of results or outcomes.

____Never   ____Sometimes   ____Always

When I have a problem, I share possible solutions with my boss.

____Never   ____Sometimes   ____Always

If you answered Never or Sometimes to even one of these questions, I invite you to continue reading and to be prepared to power up your communication.

1

COMMUNICATE WITH OOMPH

*The single biggest problem in communication
is the illusion that it has taken place.*

~ George Bernard Shaw

- ▲ Ask a strategic question
- ▲ Talk the way people listen
- ▲ Focus on the one-big-thing
- ▲ BE at the beginning and end
- ▲ Use 3 magical formulas
- ▲ Spice it up

By many standards, we've arrived. We've been invited to "sit at the table" with our male peers and senior associates to influence workplace outcomes. The problem is, we've arrived mute.

Research shows that women are not speaking up at workplace meetings as frequently as men are. We're sitting there with our hands in our laps waiting to be called on. Why is that? Men aren't raising their hands hoping the guy at the head of the table will call on them. They're jumping in feet first. They're contributing. They're letting their voices be heard.

We all know women can talk. After all, the *gift of gab* is most definitely associated with women, not men. In fact, one recent study claims that we talk more than men. Three times more, to be exact. The study reports that women speak as many as 20,000 words per day compared to the paltry 7,000 spoken by men. Many of us pride ourselves on our superior ability to communicate. We share thoughts and feelings. We tell stories.

Sure, we're a verbal tour de force when we're around our female friends and colleagues or our mothers and daughters, but something often happens when we "sit at the table." It's a fair bet that you wouldn't have been invited to the table if you didn't have something of value to add to the mix. If you want to be respected and recognized, don't just sit at the table; talk at the table! And by the way, you don't have to raise your hand. School children raise their hands; women with Leadership Presence don't.

When we contemplate contributing more actively, some tough questions immediately emerge:

- What should we choose to talk about?
- When do we talk?
- How do we talk so people listen?

If you've ever had a session with a good presentation coach, you know she spends a lot of time expounding about the importance of non-verbal communication, about the power of your body, eyes, and hands in driving home your message. I can vouch for this. I spent many years as a communication coach for top executives, and I'll certainly emphasize non-verbal communication in the next chapter. But what coaches sometimes don't tell you is that there are easy ways to optimize your verbal communication – your language – so it will have more impact, more "oomph," and so you'll be recognized as someone on her way up.

ASK A STRATEGIC QUESTION

Let's start with a simple resolution. Make it a point to contribute at least once in every meeting you attend. While it would be dreamy to consistently have a highly astute contribution, often we simply don't. If you're at a total loss for what you might contribute – or even if you are not – make it a point to ask at least one question. Your question should be a reflection of genuine interest that results from mindful listening. At its best, it will be a strategic question. A strategic question definitely qualifies as communicating with oomph.

I know some of you find the word "strategic" scary, but frankly I couldn't think of a sexier way to describe this kind of question; in fact, it should be a regular feature of your communication. If you find the notion of "strategic" intimidating or puzzling, stay with me. I'm going to take the scary out of *strategy* and put the *simple* in.

While there are a million different questions that work in countless situations, business discussions most often revolve around two basic dynamics: (1) problems and their negative impacts and (2) solutions and their positive payoffs.

Many of the women I've coached have made it to the corner office because of their ability to contribute to their firms' business strategies and to impact their bottom lines. You may not be ready to do that yet. But if your goal is advancement, you need to get cozy and comfortable with strategic thinking. Strategy has everything to do with customers, with growth, and with ROI – Return On Investment.

Your ability to ask the right strategic questions at the right time will have you well on your way up in the glass elevator. And here's the key: You don't need the answers. How easy is that? Here are some ideas for strategic questions that will get you both noticed and involved:

- ▲ Ask a question to get a handle on the general situation.
- ▲ Ask a question to get at the root of the problem.
- ▲ Ask a question about the impact of the problem.
- ▲ Ask a question about the ROI – in this case, the Risk Of Ignoring the problem. (In other words, how bad is the problem?)
- ▲ Ask a question about possible solutions.
- ▲ Ask a question about the potential payoffs for the various solutions.

Suddenly, strategy is no longer such a scary proposition. With a simple strategic question, you're becoming invested in the overriding issues of your firm. And you're prepping for an upward journey.

TALK THE WAY PEOPLE LISTEN

Now that you're committed to talking – whether with a short but sharp question or with a broad insight – the next hurdle is to talk so people will listen. This is the *how* of communicating. To improve the way we speak, however, we must first examine how people listen.

How do people listen? Well, not very well, as it turns out. Human beings are pretty poor listeners. In fact, as time passes, we are becoming less and less effective at listening. There is strong evidence that the onslaught of technology and the massive amounts of information available to us have caused our attention spans to drop significantly. Since any information we need is a click away, our memories aren't as taxed as they once were, and we can move from one subject to the next without pausing to digest.

Let's go back in time to the 1930s. Picture a family of four sitting in their living room, huddled in front of their old RCA Victor radio. Maybe they're listening to an episode of *The Green Lantern* or laughing to a *Bob Hope Comedy Special*, but in any case, they are treated to thirty minutes of programming uninterrupted by commercials or dashed by some other form of stimuli.

Fast forward to your house today and ask yourself how much it resembles the scene I just described. Try not to smile.

These days, our attention is pulled in multiple directions by various technologies that offer e-diversions and i-distractions without end: pop-ups, streaming videos, chat rooms, texts, quizzes, ads, games, and so on. You name it, it's there to divert and distract.

The average attention span in today's sound-bite world? Is it minutes? Or is it seconds?

While attention spans have decreased over time, what hasn't changed is the average attention curve. The attention curve plots an audience's ability to focus over the duration of an uninterrupted presentation, talk, speech, or lecture. Guess what? Take any of these, and it's a proven fact that people listen best at the beginning and at the end. The middle? Well, that's another story.

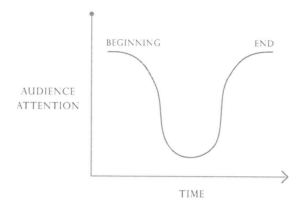

Picture yourself as a student sitting in a classroom back in high school or in a lecture hall in college. You start the class alert, pen in hand, poised to take notes. What happens? You're distracted by the cute guy in the next row. Or you find your eyes closing because you stayed up too late the night before.

Then suddenly, the teacher is wrapping up and reviewing what's going to be on the test the next day, and you're all ears. But that middle fifteen or twenty minutes? All a blur.

Think back to the last time you attended any kind of lecture. Unless the speaker was a veritable superstar (or knew the magical formulas for communicating with oomph that I'm about to share with you), I'm guessing you won't be able to tell me what she was talking about at the halfway point of her very stimulating talk. This lapse is called human nature.

This natural attention curve conveys two important lessons guaranteed to help us communicate so people actually listen: **Focus on the one-big-thing** and **BE at the Beginning and End.**

FOCUS ON THE ONE-BIG-THING

A new client of mine wanted to talk with me about an upcoming meeting with her department head and three department managers. She'd been preparing for two days for what she expected to be a fifteen-minute pitch for a new initiative. My first question to her was: "So, what's your one-big-thing?"

She started in about a new product initiative and the tactical challenges of implementing it. My eyes quickly glazed over. She didn't stop, so I stopped her.

I said, "Your boss shows up late. You glance at the clock on the wall and realize the meeting is just about over. She wants a quick summary. In the time it takes the proverbial elevator to travel from your level to the executive floor, give her your one-big-thing. What's it going to be?"

Now put yourself in my client's shoes. If you're able to deliver the one-big-thing, whether or not you have the time to elaborate, I promise you will wow your boss. She will be impressed with your clarity and succinctness. You will be perceived as a powerful communicator.

The one-big-thing is your key message. It is that one nugget you want your audience to remember, even if they forget all else.

To articulate your one-big-thing, ask:

What's the one thing I want my audience to know, think, or do after I communicate?

In meetings where you have an assigned speaking role, prepping for the one-big-thing is essential. It might sound something like this:

I want my seniors to know my team is on schedule for the June deadline.
or
I want my boss to approve my request to increase the project budget.

If you're one of many participants at a meeting, get familiar with the agenda in advance. Come prepared to contribute a one-big-thing or a key message about one item on the agenda.

BE AT THE BEGINNING AND END

Without getting too technical, the attention curve is also a memory curve, or a graphic representation of a psychological principle known as the primacy-recency theory. In other words, you and I tend to recall what's first and what's last. We remember what's at the beginning and end of a conversation or presentation with far more clarity than we do what was in the middle.

The beginning, before everyone is drowsy, is a magical opportunity to lead with your one-big-thing – that key message you want your audience to recall when the meeting is over.

Therefore, if possible, BE at the Beginning. If you contribute powerfully at the beginning of any gathering, you and your contribution will be remembered.

The end is just as critical; this is the "E" in our BE formula. It doesn't matter if someone checked out, daydreamed, or got cozy with her i-device during the middle of a meeting or presentation. She will be poised to listen at the end. Better yet, she will be poised to remember.

The best-case scenario is that you are the final speaker in any given session. When you are, the attention curve assures that you will be remembered as a powerful and integral part of the meeting.

If you are not the final speaker, and even if you weren't a major contributor during the meeting, no worries. BE at the End by jumping in and doing one of these two things:

- ▲ Articulate your own one-big-thing.
- ▲ Reiterate the one-big-thing that clearly emerged during the meeting.

CREATE YOUR OWN BEGINNING AND END

We could easily conclude our discussion by admitting that we really have only two opportunities to assert our power in any presentation, speech, meeting, or conversation: the beginning and the end. But that would be a mistake. Why? Because with a well-practiced "trick of the tongue," or by structuring your comments, you can create many beginnings and ends within any given situation.

Structuring your communication actually alters the typical dip in the attention curve. It tricks your audience into listening with full attention to multiple beginnings. The following list features a series of frameworks that allow you to effectively create two beginnings. They are:

1. FIRST and NEXT
   As in, "First, let me say this ..." followed by "Next ... you can see that ..."

2. ON THE ONE HAND and ON THE OTHER HAND
   As in, "On the one hand, the problem seems to be ..." followed by "On the other hand, you can get the same results ..."

3. PROS and CONS
   As in, "Let's take a look at the pros and cons of this situation. First, the pros ..."

4. ADVANTAGES and DISADVANTAGES
   As in, "I see both advantages and disadvantages to this solution. Let's start with the advantages ..."

5. LIKES and ADD-ONS
   As in, "Here's what I like about your plan ..." followed by "Here's what we might add to it ..."

When you use these frameworks, the listener makes a commitment after hearing the first beginning to pay attention to the second beginning. Simply put, using a two-part structure, you've successfully communicated with more oomph.

USE 3 MAGICAL FORMULAS

It is clear that structure is key in grabbing and lifting your audience's attention.

Because your ideas and perspectives are invaluable, it behooves you to communicate them so that they are both heard and respected. Concise, well-structured statements always increase your listener's comprehension and enhance your professional image. They are especially helpful in meetings with tight or stressful agendas.

The three magical formulas for communicating with oomph are:

C	CONTEXT
A	ACTION
R	RESULT

For:
- ▲ Update
- ▲ Progress
- ▲ Accomplishment

P	POINT
R	REASON
E	EXAMPLE
P	POINT

For:
- ▲ Opinion
- ▲ Idea
- ▲ Solution

C	CHALLENGE
Q	QUESTION
A	ANSWER

For:
- ▲ Challenge
- ▲ Obstacle
- ▲ Problem

CAR: CONTEXT – ACTION – RESULT

The CAR formula is perfect for delivering concise updates and subtly sharing your accomplishments.

Context. Provide context.
Action. Describe the actions you've taken.
Result. Share the results, or the impact of your actions.

The first component of the CAR formula is the **Context.** When you are providing an update about an event or situation that is important to your listener, describe the context or challenge. Set the stage ... briefly.

The second component in the CAR formula is **Action**. Communicating the action you have taken, or are currently taking, in the context you briefly described demonstrates your contribution as a leader.

We all witness men who have no trouble using the "I" word in describing the actions they've taken. Sometimes they even take full credit and beat their own chests to emphasize the point.

Women, on the other hand, tend to resort to the royal "we." Women are much more apt to share credit where credit is due, and this is a good thing. But there is also a time and place for the "I" word – when you need to make it clear what you are personally doing to make the team successful. Only by putting the "me" back in "team" can you be perceived as a leader who has impact. So don't equivocate. Bring it on.

The third component of the CAR formula is the **Result.** You want to ask yourself: What was the result of your action? What impact did your action have on the business? Was there a bottom-line result or something you can quantify? Might there be a positive outcome you expect in the future? Did you receive feedback that you can share? In communicating your result, speak the language of business. The result is built into the formula to both emphasize the business outcome and shine a spotlight on your achievements without your having to boast or brag.

This formula works magically in formal meetings when you are expected to deliver an update or explain the progress that is being made in a particular area. It also works like a charm in impromptu situations.

Use the CAR formula in formal situations

Picture yourself delivering an update at a routine meeting of your company's department heads:

(C) *My team is actively working on maximizing registration for the sales event.*

(A) *I have overseen more than half of the personal outreach and we have a 40% positive response rate to date.*

(R) *The personal touch is translating into a 20% increase in registration this year, which will give us the opportunity to market our new product more broadly.*

Or perhaps you have 30 seconds to make a positive impression in a performance review:

(C) *My biggest contribution this year was streamlining the Accounts Payable process, which was messy and costly.*

(A) *I met with the managers of our eight business units, reviewed their invoices, and demonstrated the savings they could gain by increasing the usage of our corporate credit card.*

(R) *Three of our business units have recently adopted the card and three have expanded their card usage. This has already resulted in $100,000 in savings.*

Use the CAR formula in impromptu situations

The CAR formula works equally well in informal situations. Imagine your boss poking her head into your office and asking you how that supply problem is coming along. You say:

(C) *I've been working successfully on straightening out that VizVaz Vendor situation.*

(A) *Luckily, I have an ability to be the calm in the storm and have talked them through every correction we've made.*

(R) *VizVaz actually paid me a huge compliment on our inventory management yesterday!*

Picture yourself bumping into someone important in an elevator. Consider a simple "How ya doing?" as an opportunity. Why waste time talking about the weather? Everyone already knows that it's bloody hot or friggin' cold! Instead, start with "I'm great!" And then launch into something exciting you're working on. Use the CAR formula to highlight your achievement or progress without boasting.

PREP: POINT – REASON – EXAMPLE – POINT

Being a leader doesn't mean you always need to agree with your peers or your seniors. In fact, executives are valued for the diversity of opinion they bring to the table. They're also valued for pushback that could prevent a mistake or a poor decision.

Senior leaders, both men and women alike, are valued for their opinions, ideas, and solutions.

When the men at the table are offering their ideas by being the loudest voice in the room, catch everyone's attention by offering your idea in a way that will capture them with good judgment, and do so without raising your voice. Share an opinion that separates you from your colleagues. Offer a solution that goes right to the heart of a newly identified problem.

Offer up your points in a way that is both concise and captivating by using the PREP formula:

Point. State your point or make your proposition.

Reason. Give a reason for your assertion.

Example. Provide an example or proof.

Point. Re-state your point or proposition.

Try this example on for size. You're in a meeting, and the discussion is centered on an employee named Julie and the group's concerns about her workplace demeanor. You speak up using the PREP formula to make your case.

(**P**) *Julie is a valuable employee. Instead of judging her so harshly, we should consider placing her in a marketing position that's a better match for her skills.*

(**R**) *While I agree that she still has work to do in the area of anger management, she has superb marketing capability. We've all seen her in action.*

(**E**) *I worked with her on the VizVaz account and she was great. She generated a number of creative solutions and got rave reviews from the client.*

(**P**) *I suggest we consider moving her to a marketing function.*

There it is. In less than thirty seconds, you've made your point regarding Julie, the employee in question. You've validated your reasoning in two short sentences. You've given an example that everyone in the meeting can relate to. And then you came around again and hit them with your one-line proposition.

CQA: CHALLENGE – QUESTION – ANSWER

Last in our quest to add oomph to our communication is the magical CQA formula.

Let's begin by stating an irrefutable fact: When it comes to problems and challenges, there's no difference between a CEO and a junior associate. Everyone encounters them – the difference is how we talk about them.

Women naturally process. We love to examine our days, sometimes in the most minute detail. We love to expound upon our problems, examine our bumps and bruises, and channel our annoyances. Ironically, we often go on and on about our problems even when we know how to solve them! Then, of course, we have the males in our lives who can't help jumping in with solutions, even when we're not looking for them.

This model doesn't cut it in the workplace. If you want to make it to your dream spot, you need to be a winner, not a whiner. Problem-solvers are winners. If you want to be viewed as a junior member of the team who will always remain at that level, complain away.

I'm not suggesting that you ignore the problems facing you on the job or act like you're immune to challenges. It's okay to have problems that need solving and to face difficult challenges. We all do. The twist is this: If your goal is to keep growing professionally, never bring up a challenge or articulate a problem without having at least one solution to propose.

Bottom line: Never leave home without the CQA formula in your communication arsenal. Here's how it looks:

Challenge. Share the challenge or problem you are facing without making it sound like the world is coming to an end.

Question. Concisely state the fundamental question that arises out of the challenge.

Answer. State your proposal or alternative solutions to address the situation, even if you're actually fishing for helpful input.

Picture this situation: You're a junior employee in charge of the seating arrangements for an upcoming conference. You have a problem that your boss needs to know about – a potentially crippling lack of chairs.

On the one hand, you could make yourself look like a veritable amateur by saying to her:

We don't have enough chairs for the conference! What a disaster! What am I supposed to do?

Or you could act like a junior employee with an eye on promotion by employing the CQA formula. Here's what you say instead:

(C) *We don't have enough chairs for the conference at the moment.*

(Q) *I'm trying to figure out the quickest way to get a sufficient number of extras without going over the conference budget.*

(A) *I'm thinking of asking the Accounting Group if we can borrow their extra chairs for the day or calling Facilities Management to see if there are extras in storage.*

In three concise statements, you have been clear about the challenge and made your boss feel as if the situation is under control. And you've also gotten yourself noticed.

SPICE IT UP

Let's summarize.

- Your communication needs structure.
- It needs to shine the spotlight on you.
- It must employ the language of business.

All well and good. But to truly put oomph in your communication, it needs one more thing – spice! What is the best way to do this? By sprinkling your contributions with examples, anecdotes, and stories without getting wordy or straying from the point.

The best examples and the most effective anecdotes rely on details and specifics to make them memorable long after they're told. You can do this by citing names, adding numbers, and mentioning places.

Let's return for a moment to our example about the boss who pokes her head into your office and asks you about the supply problem with VizVaz. You spice up your answer just enough by saying:

> *I got Willa Stevens, VizVaz's head of distribution, on a video conferencing call and showed her a dozen examples of the printer cartridges that were damaged. Then I described the delays the damaged goods were causing at our Lakeside warehouse. Willa said she'd get on it right away. She called earlier today and said they were shipping out 1,200 replacements via FedEx. They'll be here tomorrow by 10:00 a.m.*

Being specific but not redundant or overly detailed, you painted a picture in less than a minute that your boss can't possibly forget.

Don't forget. Women are famous for their storytelling abilities. The trick to making our spicy stories function in the workplace is to be sure they are not only short and structured, but also strategic.

An effective story resonates emotionally with your audience because it is relevant. It inspires your audience because it's fueled by your passion and relates the struggles we all face in pursuing a goal. It illustrates with a vivid example, and ultimately, it teaches an important lesson.

In thinking about your contribution to any situation or presentation, remember the limited attention span of your audience. Keep things short, structured, and relevant. But don't be afraid to add a little salt and pepper for impact! It's your own authentic spice that gives your communication oomph and makes you stand out like a leader.

THE ELEVATOR WORKOUT
COMMUNICATE WITH OOMPH

I commit to power up my communication by:

_____ Focusing on my one-big-thing

_____ Contributing more frequently

_____ Structuring my comments

_____ Using a magical formula (CAR, PREP, CQA)

_____ Adding spice

To communicate with more oomph, I will:

Stop: _____

                _____

                _____

                _____

Start: _____

                _____

                _____

                _____

Continue: _____

                _____

                _____

                _____

POWER PROFILE

$\mathcal{M}$ARY $\mathcal{B}$RIENZA

EVP & General Auditor
NYSE Euronext

As the Executive Vice-President and General Auditor of NYSE Euronext, Mary Brienza is an internationally respected executive. She is the most senior American woman at the Exchange and one of only two women who sit on its global Management Committee, a prestigious forum of the most senior decision makers.

Mary oversees global audit and risk and compliance teams comprising forty staff members. Her team includes attorneys, CPAs, and MBAs charged with assessing a wide range of risks and with auditing the worldwide operations of NYSE Euronext. It's a position that goes far beyond an expert grasp of numbers; it's a position that requires constant communication with the CEO and the Board, whose primary interest is results. It is exactly the kind of communication that demands articulating the key message of any presentation quickly and concisely.

"I have seen a lot of good, smart people stall in their careers because they talk too much or they don't get to the point," Mary says. "They don't read their audience and therefore can't convey what their audience needs to hear! You have to tailor, slice, dice, and deliver your message to succeed."

Mary wasn't always a C-level executive. She began her career as an Assistant District Attorney in New York in 1980 prosecuting violent and white-collar crimes. She was one of a few women assigned to the District Attorney's Homicide Bureau, prosecuting murder cases. This was back in the day when women couldn't wear pants in the male-dominated courtroom of detectives and judges.

"This is where I learned to communicate," Mary says. "Back then, I might have ten minutes to weed out obviously biased jurors during jury selection. I listened to every word a potential juror said and observed every facial expression while the judge was questioning them. I had to make it all count when it was my turn to talk."

In the courtroom, Mary recalls that she had all of thirty seconds to make a positive first impression. She discovered that the pre-written list of questions in her briefcase could turn out to be her worst enemy. Mary learned to improvise, to think on her feet, and to change directions as she read her audience, all skills she uses every day in her current job. "You have to pay attention. You have to listen before you speak. And when you have something to say, dare to speak."

In 1992, Mary took a risk when she joined the Division of Enforcement for the NYSE, litigating matters against member firms for violations of exchange rules and federal securities laws. With no experience in stocks or bonds, she learned on the job and prospered. After ten years, she jumped to the business side of the exchange and began conducting internal audits on the regulatory program she had just worked for. Then, when the NYSE and Euronext merged in 2007, she was promoted to her current position.

It may sound like it all came easily, but it didn't. Mary saw her office in the World Trade Center destroyed on 9/11. She is also a cancer survivor.

Adversity, she will tell you, has made her stronger. It has given her perspective. As a result, she has become a better manager, a more effective leader, and a fully-focused mother to four daughters to boot. In an executive position where crisis and confrontation are facts of life, she rarely gets rattled or upset.

"When you remain calm," she says, "you find the give and take of communication is easy."

So what advice does Mary have for women who want to move upward? "Be open to trying things outside your comfort zone. This might mean a lateral move or even a slight loss in status. Remember that different things take you down different paths, and that's where you'll find growth. Be responsible for your own career and look out for yourself. Seek out the appropriate training when you need it, and plan for where you want to be in a year, in three years, in five years."

THE GROUND FLOOR QUIZ
STRUT YOUR STUFF

When I dress in the morning, I think about whom I am going to meet.

____Never   ____Sometimes   ____Always

I sit in meetings in a way that shows I am interested and engaged.

____Never   ____Sometimes   ____Always

I shake hands firmly, with men and women alike.

____Never   ____Sometimes   ____Always

I know what to do with my hands when I speak.

____Never   ____Sometimes   ____Always

I am comfortable making eye contact when I am speaking or listening.

____Never   ____Sometimes   ____Always

I am careful to monitor my facial expressions when I disagree with someone.

____Never   ____Sometimes   ____Always

If you answered Never or Sometimes to even one of these questions, I invite you to continue reading and to be prepared to power up your executive presence.

$\mathcal{S}$TRUT YOUR $\mathcal{S}$TUFF

It has nothing to do with clothing or makeup.
Just put your shoulders back and chin up, and face the world with pride.

~ Helen Mirren

- ▲ Power up your dress
- ▲ Power up your moves
- ▲ Power up your face
- ▲ Power up your hands
- ▲ Power up your voice

Women have a distinct advantage in the workplace. Women are beautiful.

Let's do an experiment. Randomly select a hundred women off the street and put them in a room together. Then do the same with a hundred men and gather them in the room next door. Now call in a completely objective panel of judges; in fact, we'll get a group of androgynous evaluators from Mars. Their job is to survey both rooms and determine which has more beautiful people in it. Androgynous or not, it's a no-brainer. The room filled with the one hundred women would win hands down every time. Ask our judges which room has the most regal presence. Same answer. The most discerning gazes and inspiring smiles? Easy.

Women are indeed beautiful. While the "fairer sex" brings a great deal more to the table than loveliness, women throughout history have been recognized more for their physically appealing traits than for their intelligence and power. Let's simply acknowledge that the world has not always been even-handed.

Today, female beauty is still highly regarded, but we are now more frequently recognized for our courage, wisdom, and influence. This long overdue attitude adjustment has contributed to our recognition in the political arena as well as the corporate one. Women are more than merely aesthetically pleasing. Women are brainy. We are exceptional relationship builders. We possess remarkable leadership skills.

Yet the possession of these broad capabilities doesn't always constitute the whole of how we're judged. Some women – and men, too – also benefit from the widely researched "halo effect." If you've ever fantasized about having a halo (or wished that people could actually see yours!), this is news you've been waiting for. The halo effect is the result of a proven cognitive bias, a deviation from rational judgment that we each employ in particular situations. It states that we have a tendency to attribute a certain trait to a person simply because he or she demonstrates another. In short, we tend to think that attractive people have more desirable personalities and better skill sets than people of average appearance.

You may have heard the story of the female research subject who interviews twice for the same job using the same resume, responding to the interviewer's questions with identical answers. In one interview, she is groomed and dressed with impeccable style. In the second, she disguises herself as unattractive and unkempt. Guess who is judged consistently as the more intelligent and capable candidate? Interviewee #1, hands down.

The point is not about which woman was judged to be more beautiful. Rather, I use this story to illustrate the power of attentive executive presence. What does this mean for you? Simply that in the workplace, you should always present your most polished self. If this lends to someone's positive view of you, then prove that bias to be spot-on correct.

But attractiveness accounts for only one aspect of strutting our stuff. Non-verbal communication plays a vital role as well.

It is widely understood that we communicate in multiple ways. Albert Mehrabian, a psychology professor long known for spearheading communication research, coined the famed three Vs of communication: verbal, vocal, and visual – the three elements that most influence how we perceive people when they are communicating. Do we like what they are saying or are we put off by it? Are we engaged or indifferent? Galvanized or bored? And frankly, do we like the person or not?

Here's how it works. A person's words – what we call *verbal* – account for a mere 7% of our perception of them. Tone of voice – what we call *vocal* – accounts for 38% of our reaction. Body language – what we call *visual* – accounts for a full 55% of our response. This is a remarkable finding. What it means is that a whopping 93% of our perception and understanding of others is attributed to non-verbal characteristics like volume, intonation, stance, gestures, and eye contact.

THE 3 ELEMENTS OF COMMUNICATION

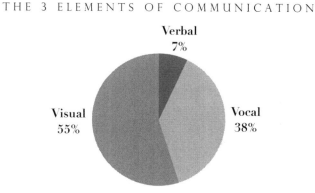

A powerful illustration of this was reflected in a study in which non-verbal cues, such as physical posture, had four times the effect of verbal cues in causing someone to appear dominant. That example alone exhibits how non-verbal communication is precisely the kind of tool we can use to maximize our allure as leaders. It is therefore prudent to remember that on your way up in the elevator, the words you choose may not be as important as the subtle elements that accompany them.

In particular, let's examine the powerful impact your visual and vocal cues can have on those around you.

POWER UP YOUR DRESS

When it comes to dress, I hate rules. I went to parochial schools, and the people in charge were notorious for insisting that their minions wear uniforms. In high school, I had to wear the same plaid skirt every single day. I loathed it. I can't tell you how often I came to school wearing a more teen-friendly skirt, proclaiming to anyone who would listen that my uniform was "in the wash." The truth is, if I had actually laundered that poor garment as often as I claimed to, it would have disintegrated by winter break. When I did wear it, I rolled the hem up – showing far too much leg and driving my principal to distraction – and paired it with a jean shirt for the cool factor and a red bandana for a touch of attitude. A rebel at heart.

Even then, I saw fashion as a way of making statements, some good, some not so good, but statements nonetheless. When I graduated with an MBA from Columbia Business School, I readily admit that I looked with genuine boredom at my graduating mates' black interview suits. *Not me*, I thought. I showed up at an interview at Proctor & Gamble in Cincinnati, Ohio in an olive Tahari suit and purple stockings. I looked great, just not for the occasion at hand. And I paid the price. I lost out on the marketing position I was pursuing even before I opened my mouth. I had more luck with the same outfit, however, at fashion-forward L'Oreal in New York; they loved my style and offered me a much-sought-after position in their marketing department.

Needless to say, I learned an invaluable lesson from these experiences. It was the juxtaposition of those two interviews that seeded the notion of just how loudly dress speaks. I discovered with certainty that it's never too early to ask yourself this question: Are you dressing for yourself or for the job you want?

MAKE THE RIGHT STATEMENT

Like some of you, I am soon to launch my own kids into what I hope are successful, sustaining careers.

"The interns wear jeans," my daughter says to me.

"If you just want the internship," I tell her, "wear the jeans. If you want the job that follows the internship, we're going shopping tomorrow for slacks and blazers."

The choice, as I told her, was hers, but I wanted her to know how important these decisions were right from the get-go. It's the same for every woman. It doesn't matter what your position is in the workplace. Dress for the job you really want. Make a statement, but make sure it's the right statement.

When it comes to dress, successful women make their own rules. But they also know that their audience provides the guidelines in every given situation. You can choose between a Bebe cleavage-revealing top or a two-piece Theory suit and look fantastic in both. But first, know your audience and the guidelines it dictates.

The successful woman never gets dressed in the morning without first considering the following:

Who am I going to meet today? What are their expectations? Formal or informal? Businesslike or casual?

What kind of impression am I intending to make? Casual and friendly? Creative and edgy? Professional and mature?

Once you answer those questions, go ahead and make the rules. Dress to meet expectations and to create the right impression. Choose the outfit. Set the guidelines for your hairstyle, make-up, accessories, shoes, and even your nails. Every decision you make serves to communicate a memorable personal brand to your audience.

POWER UP YOUR MOVES

Successful women move with confidence. They have what we call executive presence: the aplomb and capability that all successful and high-potential executives exude.

When you walk into a room, rest assured that people are unconsciously filling the blackboard of their brains with adjectives that describe you either positively or negatively. What is a new client thinking? What are your new hires seeing? In that first moment, are they considering you to be polished and professional? Blasé and uninspiring? Scattered and sloppy?

Make no mistake about it: First impressions are powerful. First impressions last. And your appearance, carriage, and mannerisms are the first attributes people notice.

POSTURE, POSITION & PROJECTION

The last thing you want in the workplace – or anywhere for that matter – is to be perceived as a wimpy woman. These women slouch. They stare at the floor. They fold their arms or clutch their hands across their bodies in a "fig leaf" position, the way a young girl does when her parents are chastising her. Their bodies are shouting, *I am not confident. I am not capable.*

Juxtapose this image against that of the successful woman, a leader who knows her place in the world. What do you see? She plants her feet, stands tall and relaxed, and makes eye contact with every person with whom she interacts. Her hands are relaxed at her sides, ready to power up in an instant. "Tower, don't cower," author Sam Horn advocates.

On that note, imagine yourself walking the corridors at your workplace. Stride with assurance, as if you have an invisible strand of pearls extending along your spine – gracefully, comfortably, engagingly. When you stop moving, don't stop exuding. Even sitting down, you can project confidence.

Picture yourself in a group meeting, even one in which you are more observer than participant. It doesn't matter what your role is; you're still being watched. This is no time to lean back in your chair, chug your diet coke, or check out the chips in your nail polish. You have the ability to look powerful even if you don't open your mouth. You can exude executive presence by sitting comfortably between the middle and edge of your chair, feet flat on the ground, shoulders leaning forward slightly, with your hands relaxed. The more you power up your posture, the more people around you will see you as someone ready to connect and to contribute bigger things in more valuable ways.

POWER UP YOUR FACE

Contrary to what you may be thinking, this section is not about applying cosmetics. Although I must say, we women are lucky. Makeup is a blessing. Having lost the dewy shine of youth, I find a touch of makeup goes a long way in fortifying my look and giving me an energetic glow. And if you're approaching what I call the "middle years" as I am, I highly recommend a drop of makeup for a polished, professional look.

But cosmetics aside, what I am really talking about is the ability to use your countenance and eyes to connect. Because the human face is blessed with nineteen major facial muscles, humans have the developed ability to maximize their expression more than any other creature on earth. Use it. A simple way to begin is with the smile, the most universal of all signs of warmth and welcome. A smile invites engagement and connection with other people, and because smiling is a feel-good action, people tend to respond in kind.

Next, stay aware of your expression. When someone else is speaking, what exactly is your face doing? Your facial expression is an open door to your thoughts and feelings. When you're bored with a speaker, do you sigh and glance away? When you're irritated, do you grimace or roll your eyes?

Unspoken feedback can be quite loud and insulting. Regardless of your level of interest or agreement, resist the urge to show signs of impatience, annoyance, or apathy. Instead, give the speaker respect by nodding your head and making eye contact.

ENGAGE WITH YOUR EYES

Eye contact is your ticket to credibility and should, in fact, be a consistent, constant, and continuous part of your presence. Western audiences want you to "look them in the eye" – we see it as a mark of honesty and forthrightness. In contrast, if someone is described as "shifty-eyed" or "beady-eyed," he or she is being labelled as untrustworthy. If you're a parent, you may catch yourself saying to your children, "Look me in the eye when you tell me that." Why? Because if they can't, they're probably fudging the truth!

Studies have proven what we intuitively know is true. We're better at eye contact than men. While we women in Western society can maintain eye contact 100% of the time during informal conversation, men only sustain it an average of 80%. This knowledge creates a prime opportunity for you to adjust to the difference and leverage your strength.

And one-on-one conversation is not the only arena in which eye contact counts. Think of instances when you are the speaker. You will indisputably appear more confident and powerful if you look at your audience while you talk. You will certainly be more compelling. The added bonus is that you will also be able to gauge audience reaction by using your natural affinity with eye contact to connect, to gather information, to interpret signals, and to adjust your communication.

By the same token, when you're a listener among a group, be sure to make eye contact with the person speaking at any given time. Leave your i-device – whichever one you happen to favor – at your desk. Your ability to listen and attend to others with your eyes is a vital, irreplaceable part of your executive presence.

The same advice holds true for making effective eye contact with a group of people. Think of having "mini-conversations" – look at one person long enough to complete a thought or phrase, and then move on to another face. With a little concentrated effort on your part, each person in your presence will feel valued and connected with you.

POWER UP YOUR HANDS

People are drawn to the magnetism of a powerful communicator. Much of that perceived power comes from hands, the vehicles that make words come alive. Firm, emphatic gestures animate a conversation and convey confidence.

Picture a conductor's hands: one moment firm, the next coaxing; one moment intent, the next lilting, but always the hands of leadership.

We all use gestures – even on the phone when no one can see us. The trick is to incorporate the same unconscious, relaxed style of gesturing in more formal presentation and communication at work, using your hands to animate and emphasize.

Do:
- ▲ Shoot energy all the way to the ends of your fingertips.
- ▲ Use small gestures in tight spaces.
- ▲ Expand your gestures and arm movements in large spaces.
- ▲ "Draw" what you're talking about with your hands.
- ▲ Vary your gestures.

Don't:
- ▲ Cross your arms over your chest.
- ▲ Clasp your fingers tightly.
- ▲ Repeat any single gesture frequently.
- ▲ Twiddle your wedding ring or necklace.
- ▲ Play with your hair.

FIRM UP YOUR HANDSHAKE

There was a time when femininity involved a woman placing her hand gently into the hand of another upon meeting or departing. Thankfully, that time has passed. But some women still offer a wimpy hand. It can feel a bit like a dead fish. *Ugh.* The handshake is part of your first impression, so be aware that a limp wrist or the partial grasp of another's hand leaves a weak perception of you.

If this is your tendency, there's an easy remedy. In fact, I suggest you practice it with a friend to get some feedback. Extend your hand, clasping the other person's entire hand with a strong momentary squeeze. Simultaneously, connect eye-to-eye, then release. Voilà!

With that one simple but powerful action, you have made a first and lasting impression as a strong, poised, and confident woman.

POWER UP YOUR VOICE

It was the Sirens in Greek mythology who lured sailors with their enchanting voices, causing countless shipwrecks on the rocky coast of their island. While they were not purely human – in fact, avian traits have often been attributed to Sirens – and their exact creature-hood has been the subject of scholarly debate, they were indisputably women. And we do know that their voices were beautiful and enchanting.

The power of voice is extraordinary. We've all been captivated by certain voices: Winston Churchill, James Earl Jones, Katharine Hepburn, Maya Angelou, to name a few. Their voices resonate, carry weight, and are memorable for their tone and timbre. Even if you're not genetically gifted in the vocal department, there's much you can do to develop the voice of a leader.

GO FROM GIRL TO WOMAN

When it comes to pitch, women favor the higher ranges while men favor the lower. Yet you'll rarely find a squeaky girl-like voice among women in the executive suite. Is there anything you can do if your natural tone is a bit high?

The good news is: yes! Experiment by imagining you're a queen speaking down to her subjects from the castle balcony. Utilize the lower ranges that carry with them a sense of gravitas, something your subjects would expect.

Next, become aware of your intonation. A major girl-problem is the upward inflection that makes every sentence sound like a question. This is the sound of uncertainty, the absolute last impression you want to leave. Research tells us that the voice of authority utilizes a downward inflection. But downward does not mean petering out; stay strong right to the end of each sentence. Strong finishes convey confidence, and confidence conveys power.

WHOA GIRL

Chatter-mouth and *gift of gab* are phrases long associated with women. Some of us have the ability to talk a mile a minute. There may be a time and a place for this, but it's not the workplace. When you slow down, you're perceived as more thoughtful, giving the listener time to both receive and process the information. At the same time, keep in mind the value of altering your pace periodically. You might tell a story a bit faster; you might slow it down a notch when explaining data or complex information. Sometimes even incorporating a pregnant pause – a precisely placed moment of silence – can have an incredible impact.

Your voice is beautiful, especially when it's laced with confidence. New research from Professor Ernesto Rubin of Columbia Business School suggests that male domination in the C-suite may be partially due to men's natural overconfidence in their business performance, which is often conveyed verbally. Men frequently give the impression from the start that they cannot fail, simply by how they speak. Why shouldn't women exude the same level of self-assurance?

Yes, it can be scary to give a speech or a presentation in front of a crowded room, and yes, it can be intimidating when you have the floor in an important meeting. But these are perfect opportunities for powering up your executive presence. Start by being completely comfortable with your message. Know your audience. Know your material. And then project with confidence.

You have all the stuff. Now go out and strut it.

THE ELEVATOR WORKOUT

STRUT YOUR STUFF

I commit to power up my executive presence with my:

_____ Dress

_____ Moves

_____ Face

_____ Hands

_____ Voice

To strut my stuff, I will:

Stop: _____

_____

_____

_____

Start: _____

_____

_____

_____

Continue: _____

_____

_____

_____

POWER PROFILE

*N*ANCY *M*CKINSTRY

Chief Executive Officer
Wolters Kluwer

Nancy McKinstry uses the term "superior results" to describe what she has always aspired to deliver during her career. She says: "I never chased a promotion. I just focused on doing a superior job. I always did more than what I was asked to do."

As CEO and Chairman of the Executive Board of Wolters Kluwer, her efforts have earned her a place on *Fortune*'s 2011 Global 50 Most Powerful Women in Business and Financial Times' Top 50 Women in World Business. "I have to say that I've always gravitated toward leadership roles. I always wanted to be at the top. I was the kind of girl who wanted to get straight As in school."

Wolters Kluwer, a Dutch-based global information provider, may not be a household name in the US, but it is a market-leading information services and publishing company with 19,000 employees, offices in 45 countries, and customers all over the world. Its CEO began her working career when she was just thirteen years old, doing chores in the kitchen of a local summer camp. She had more jobs than she can remember while she was putting herself through college.

"If you're waiting for someone else to figure out the best way for you to succeed, you're in trouble." She easily adds, however, that there were plenty of wonderful people along the way who helped her and taught her the value of mentorship and sponsorship.

After graduating from the University of Rhode Island with a degree in Economics and Political Science, Nancy earned an MBA in finance and marketing at Columbia University. She went to work for Booz Allen Hamilton, an international management-consulting firm and soon after took a job with CCH, working her way up through the ranks to become the President and CEO of Legal Information Services. The stage was set for her emergence with Wolters Kluwer when the company purchased CCH, and Nancy began running the North American operation. In 2003, she was named CEO of the entire company and now lives with her family in the Netherlands. A roller coaster ride to be sure, but one driven by a philosophy of doing superior work day in and day out without exception.

"The higher you are in an organization, the less it is about you," Nancy says. "It is more about your ability to create and express a vision. It is more about bringing a team of people together to execute that vision. As a leader, you set the path, then you empower your team with tools to navigate that path to get where you want them to go."

This is the foundation of Nancy's leadership model. She likens leadership at the top to that of the music director of a jazz band. "You have to know your players' strengths and weaknesses, and you have to make sure the music benefits from the former and doesn't suffer from the latter."

She candidly shares her own weaknesses. She claims that she was not a born communicator but had to learn the art. "Every culture has a different way of communicating. The more global you are, the more diverse the identities. The Netherlands is a consensus culture. In the US, it's a 'getting-it-done' culture. But everyone wants to be heard, and everyone wants to be respected. That's universal."

When it comes to her team, Nancy hires smart people who know what it means to overcome adversity. "I want people who can rise to the occasion when things get tough."

And sure enough, most of the people who now hold senior positions in Nancy's company are people she hired long ago. "I am very direct with my people about what I expect from them. We set goals, we review those goals every month, and we work side by side to reach those goals. I am a believer in working collectively to make things better."

On the other hand, Nancy does not believe in beating around the bush. "I believe in giving feedback, good and bad. I give praise as well as constructive criticism. I'm not shy about saying things that produce a negative reaction. The members of any team need to hear from their leader about their performance, about what they're doing and not doing."

Nancy's message to women who want to ride the glass elevator to the top is very straightforward: "Do two things. One, focus on delivering superior results in your current role. Ask your boss what the top three things are that you have to work on to get better and how they can be measured. Two, talk about your superior results. Talk about what you're doing for your business. In other words, toot your own horn. Do this, and you'll get the promotion you're looking for."

When asked if she ever viewed being a woman as either an advantage or a disadvantage, Nancy is quick to say: "I don't believe being a woman ever had an impact on my ability to perform or ever impeded my progress. I believe if you really want a career, you can do it, whether you are a woman or a man. Gender and competition have less to do with it than your own passion, skills, and dedication."

THE GROUND FLOOR QUIZ
LISTEN LIKE A LEADER

I encourage others to speak by nodding or using sounds like *uh-huh*.

____Never   ____Sometimes   ____Always

I delay offering my opinion until I hear what others have to say.

____Never   ____Sometimes   ____Always

I ask questions to learn more.

____Never   ____Sometimes   ____Always

I paraphrase others' comments.

____Never   ____Sometimes   ____Always

I let a speaker know that I grasp the strong emotions she's conveying.

____Never   ____Sometimes   ____Always

I succinctly summarize the key points of discussions at meetings.

____Never   ____Sometimes   ____Always

If you answered Never or Sometimes to even one of these questions, I invite you to continue reading and to be prepared to power up your listening.

$\mathscr{L}$ISTEN LIKE A $\mathscr{L}$EADER

*We have two ears and one mouth
so that we can listen twice as much as we speak.*

~ Epictetus, Greek Philosopher

▲ Attach both ears
▲ Open the door
▲ Don't slam the door
▲ 3 ways to talk while you listen
▲ Monitor your balance

Communicating with oomph is a twofold skill. Savvy women know not only when to *talk* but also when to *listen*. They know not only *how* to talk but also *how* to listen. In other words, they know how to balance advocacy and acknowledgement.

When you advocate, you share your position, advise, or problem-solve. When you acknowledge, you open your mind to new information, new possibilities, and new avenues of thought. In short, you listen to learn.

When you listen to learn, you listen like a leader. When you listen like a leader, you are perceived as one. As with so many things in life, however, listening openly and actively is easier said than done.

How many times have you stopped yourself in the middle of a sentence and looked across the table at your kids or mate and said, "You're not listening!" How many times have you wanted to say that at work? You're not alone.

It's not a surprise that we can easily be distracted. Human beings speak at a rate of 100–200 words per minute. That's a lot of words to process in sixty seconds. I'm a New Yorker, and we New Yorkers are famous for hitting the high end of that range. If you're a southerner, your claim to fame is a slower, less frenetic way of speaking. But we can all think quicker than anyone can talk. If our thoughts were measured in words, the rate would be 400–500 words per minute. We often think about our next verbal assault instead of listening to what someone else is saying.

You know how it goes. We might be thinking about the call we forgot to make to the doctor, the sushi we want for lunch, or how the laundry is piling up at home. We might be mulling over an alternative strategy for a product launch, what we're going to say during a conference call later that day, or jumping two steps ahead in the conversation that's taking place right then and there.

While the gap between the rate of speech (100–200 words per minute) and the rate of thought (400–500 words per minute) can be a distraction, it can also be a source of tremendous power. When we listen with two ears intent on learning, we listen actively to what's being said as well as to what's *not* being said. We can pay attention to the emotion behind the speaker's words and evaluate what pieces of information we want or need to understand better.

Traditional wisdom suggests that the best and most effective way to listen is with our mouths shut. It is true that silence on the part of the listener encourages the speaker to proceed at her own pace and elaborate more fully. But listening in total silence is like a state of nirvana. May we all attain it.

We're not very good at keeping our mouths shut for long periods of time. It just doesn't seem to be in our nature. And the amount of training it would take to reprogram this natural state of being would be enormous. It is a rare occasion when any of us can listen for extended periods of time without some measure of verbal response.

Our best bet is to use our nature to our advantage. With that in mind, let's talk about a listening model that doesn't torture you by timing your stints of silence down to the second or stretch you to the point of bursting like a geyser. I call it *listening like a leader*. Powerful leaders know how to meld talking with listening sensitively, and by the end of this chapter, you'll know how to do it too.

When you listen effectively, you give much needed comfort and recognition to the speaker. At the same time, you benefit yourself by gaining clarity and knowledge. In other words, you learn. Most important, effective listening helps you build the kind of powerful and sustainable relationships that aid your professional ascent.

Knowing when to kick in this advanced form of listening is tricky at first. Instinct plays a key role. Women are generally far more instinctive than men, so we have a head start.

Begin by noting the type of occasions that call for a heightened state of listening:

- ▲ When you hear a new idea
- ▲ When someone offers an opinion that is different from yours
- ▲ Before you move into action
- ▲ Before you share your own experience
- ▲ Before you argue or criticize
- ▲ When the other person is experiencing strong feelings
- ▲ When the other person wants to talk over a problem
- ▲ When the other person is having difficulty expressing herself

Once you recognize the situation, step away from the convention of listen-talk-listen-talk (or for some people: listen-talk-talk-talk-talk-talk). How do we do this?

ATTACH BOTH EARS

Metaphorically speaking, when both ears are attached, you give yourself the gift of curiosity, which is priceless for any leader, and you can probe without interrupting. When your interest is obvious, the speaker is encouraged to continue. You then grasp what is being said with greater clarity and engage positively.

But sometimes it's impossible to be fully engaged, isn't it? Take for example those moments when you have to choose between completing a critical email and a conversation with someone on your team who has shown up at your desk.

Your best strategy is to let her know that you'll get to her as soon as both ears are attached again. Here is a magical response that can be tweaked to fit almost any occasion:

Hey, what you're saying is really important and demands my full attention. Can we talk about it in 15 minutes after I respond to this?

And just an FYI for all you parents: If you find yourself saying "not now" or "can't you see I'm busy!" to your kids at home, a similar line works wonders:

It sounds like you have really great things to share. Mommy's going to finish this phone call and then I'm going to give you both of my ears!

Once you're committed to fully engage, create an environment with as few distractions as possible and a minimum number of barriers between the two of you.

A few suggestions:

- ▲ Lose the i-device.
- ▲ Face your colleague.
- ▲ Come out from behind your desk.
- ▲ Create the appropriate distance between you.
- ▲ Look 'em in the eye with the intent of sending the message:
  I'm interested in what you have to say.

OPEN THE DOOR

A door opener is a verbal or non-verbal device that invites a person to speak and shows her your willingness to engage.

Picture a colleague coming by your office and peeking in with one of those *can-I-have-a-word* expressions on her face. In other words, she wants your ear (or two ears, to be more exact). You invite her in with a

'What's up?" or a "Have a seat," and you've successfully employed a door opener.

As she's speaking, a smile, a nod, or an *uh-huh* all send the message *I hear you.*

On the other hand, if you interrupt or jump in with a response before your colleague has finished whatever it is she came to see you about in the first place, you effectively fail Listen Like a Leader 101.

DON'T SLAM THE DOOR

For every door opener, you can bet there are two or three door slammers that can put a sudden and immediate end to a conversation or an interaction and keep you stuck on the first floor.

Listening is challenging enough. It gets even tougher when the content is difficult to hear or when it is laden with emotion. It gets even more difficult when what we're hearing makes us uncomfortable or when we are emotionally involved with the speaker.

If things get too difficult, what happens? We put up barriers that prevent true sharing or understanding. Any chance of engaging on a deep level evaporates into thin air. We sometimes unintentionally slam the door on an opportunity for successful interaction.

There are three classic door slammers that we all fall victim to: **judging, avoiding,** and **advising**.

JUDGING

We judge when we don't have all the facts or when we're biased toward a certain point of view. When we judge, we say things like:

- ▲ *Why the heck did you do that? What were you thinking?*
- ▲ *She's a bitch. You're a princess compared to her.*
- ▲ *You've got no one else to blame for this mess but yourself.*
- ▲ *You made a bad decision. There's no other way to look at it.*

AVOIDING

We avoid when we don't want to get involved or when we don't want to make the effort. When we avoid, we say things like:

- ▲ *Don't worry about it. It will all work out in the end.*
- ▲ *You think you've got it bad? Let me tell you what happened to me!*
- ▲ *I'm the last person you want to be discussing that with, believe me.*
- ▲ *Cheer up. It's not the end of the world.*

ADVISING

We advise when our guidance hasn't been asked for, when our advice isn't required, or when we jump to conclusions. When we advise, we say things like:

- ▲ *You should march in there and demand what's rightfully yours.*
- ▲ *If I were you, I'd tell him off in no uncertain terms.*
- ▲ *Let me tell you what I did when I was in this situation.*
- ▲ *No sweat. Here's what you do.*

If you can hear yourself saying any of these things, or making other comments from your own personal list of judging, avoiding, or advising – and who doesn't have her own list – let me offer you some alternative ways to talk while you listen.

THREE WAYS TO TALK WHILE YOU LISTEN

1	ASK QUESTIONS
2	PARAPHRASE
3	EMPATHIZE

ASK QUESTIONS

We ask questions to check our understanding of what's being said and to learn more. Duh! This sounds so obvious. The problem is not the theory, but the execution. Sometimes we phrase our questions poorly or ask the wrong ones. Sometimes we ask too many questions or even interrogate.

When you focus on using open-ended questions that require more than one-word answers, you will engage more productively with your co-workers.

The Open-Ended Question

Open-ended questions are the type that don't allow the speaker the chance to answer with a single word or a well-placed grunt. They give her the space she needs to explore the subject at hand.

Picture this. You walk into your boss's office and ask, "Did you think my report was okay?" This is a classic example of a closed question that encourages a monosyllabic answer. You get a grunt at minimum and "'twas fine" at maximum. That's not what you came into her office hoping to hear.

On the other hand, if you use an open-ended question like, "What are your thoughts regarding my report?" you crack open an incredible opportunity for sharing and learning. An open-ended question encourages the speaker's participation and allows you to build on a relationship that may prove to be vital in your glass elevator ride.

Put these five ridiculously easy open-ended questions in your listening repertoire and you'll be amazed at the results:

- ▲ *I'd like to understand your perspective.*
- ▲ *Tell me more about that.*
- ▲ *How do you see it?*
- ▲ *What's behind that?*
- ▲ *What else?*

The Anti-Listening Question

There's an old saying that goes: "There's no such thing as a bad question." Don't believe it. There are plenty of bad questions, and the worst of these is what I call the anti-listening question. It's the *I-don't-really-want-to-listen-to-your-answer* sentiment, hiding behind a question mark. This is the type of question that causes the speaker to shut down, sometimes completely. It's the kind that discourages sharing and puts a serious damper on your learning.

We've all asked these questions, and we've all been on the receiving end of them. They sometimes begin with phrases like: "Don't tell me..." "Why in the world..." and "How can you explain..."

The **Leading Question** is a classic anti-listening question. This is the type of question phrased to suggest a desired answer. Revisiting our previous example about you, your boss, and the report you've written, the obvious leading question would be: "So, did you like my report?" You are, of course, trying to draw out a positive response, such as: "Oh, I thought it was terrific," rather than soliciting input and encouraging discussion.

I suggest making a study of this at home where your guard is down and the tendency to ask leading questions is at its highest, especially around kids.

Some time back, when my daughter returned home from yet another Bar Mitzvah party, I went straight into my bag of leading questions and asked, "So, did you have fun?" Bad move.

What could she say? The question communicated the expectation that, of course, she had fun. Five short words and I had instantaneously created a barrier preventing her from communicating openly with me about the miserable time she had. The open-ended alternative, "Tell me about it," might have sounded like a more genuine offer of generous listening from me. Believe me, breaking down a communication barrier can be more difficult than putting it up.

Very often, the leading questions we use at work are subtler than the one I asked my daughter, and we may not even be aware of using them. The antidote is to listen closely, not only to others, but also to yourself.

Another anti-listening question is the **Forced Choice Question**. This requires the speaker to choose between two available options. Similar in many ways to the closed question, a forced choice question encourages the speaker neither to expound nor to participate. When I get home from work and ask my husband, "Do you want Indian or Chinese tonight?" I have clearly limited his input with a forced choice question. Of course, I will admit that this comes in handy at times!

But returning to our example once again, you say to your boss, "So, what did you think of my report? Good or bad?"

What happened to the gray area? What happened to the open-ended invitation to learn about how your report was effective and where it could be even more effective? In one simple question, you discouraged productive feedback and demonstrated a lack of interest in truly learning.

PARAPHRASE

How often would you swear that someone said something, only to have her totally deny it ("I did NOT say that!")? As the clever writer Robert McCloskey once put it, "I know that you believe you understand what you think I said, but I'm not sure you realize that what you heard is not what I meant."

The answer to this conundrum of "he said, she said" is the paraphrase.

To paraphrase means to reword or restate something in your own words. And effective paraphrasing ensures a meeting of the minds. Imagine yourself in conversation with a colleague. She's talking; you're listening like a leader. When she's finished, you paraphrase what she's said to reflect her meaning. And trust me, if you get it wrong, she'll let you know. That's why we do it: to check our understanding and encourage the speaker to elaborate so that we gain further clarity.

With those goals in mind, here are some very useful segues into paraphrasing to store in your communication arsenal:

- *Let me make sure I understand what you are saying…*
- *If I hear you right, what you're saying is that…*
- *Help me understand. If I hear you correctly…*
- *So what I heard you say is that…, right?*

Paraphrasing is a listening skill that you'll hear at the highest levels of leadership. But it's also that little thing you can do to assert your power in a meeting where your role is more observer than contributor. In longer meetings or seminars you can have the same impact by adding summative statements at obvious transitions or at the end.

For example:

Let's recap the ground we've covered so far…
Let's stop for a second and make sure we're all on the same page…
Let's review for a moment…

In all cases, your goal is twofold: to contribute to the team effort and to present yourself as a woman meant for something higher.

EMPATHIZE

The ability to empathize is the last of our *Three Ways to Talk While You Listen*. Empathy is classically defined as the capability to identify with or vicariously experience the thoughts, feelings, or experiences of another. Not a bad gift to have.

You've probably heard the term Emotional Intelligence popping up in the workplace. Corporate leaders in industries and organizations nationwide are recognizing the development of Emotional Intelligence as a vehicle for change, and empathy is one of its component skills.

With this in mind, guess who has the greatest capacity for expressing empathy? You know the answer, because you can feel it in your gut. Women's ability to experience and identify with the emotions of others far exceeds the male population's, hands down. While I personally don't need scientific proof, a 2009 study showed that even at a younger age, girls score far higher in their ability to "stand in another's shoes" than boys. Girls can sense trouble. They can also sense need. They empathize far more than boys do.

That same skill we had when we were girls on the playground gives us power in the workplace. When we listen empathically, we absorb what people are saying and how they are saying it – the tone of their voice, the look in their eyes – and gain an understanding of what they are feeling and why. We do more than increase the accuracy of comprehension. We also promote trust and collaboration, two highly sought and valued traits in senior leadership.

Empathic listening begins with observation.

Listen with Your Eyes

As you focus on somebody who is speaking, be careful not to jump to any unjustified conclusion. Any one gesture or body movement may not reflect the true attitude of the speaker – you can't take a single movement and measure emotion.

To read non-verbal communication accurately, you have to consider the cues in **context**; you have to observe them in **clusters**; and you have to look for **congruence** with the speaker's language.

Context:

When you're listening like a leader, it is vital that you read non-verbal signals in the context in which they are happening. For example, is the speaker who has her arms and legs tightly crossed having negative thoughts or is she merely reacting to a cranked-up air conditioner?

Clusters:

There is often a tendency to take a gesture, like an open palm or a person readjusting in her seat, and read it in isolation. Don't fall for this. Look instead for cues in readable clusters for more accurate insight into a speaker's feelings. I have found that clusters of three are the most telling. For example, someone who is reacting negatively to your idea might have her arms and legs tightly crossed, her fist over her mouth, *and* her head and chin in a downward position.

Congruence:

Congruence, with regard to listening and learning, refers to verbal and non-verbal cues that are similar or in sync. In other words, if a speaker claims she agrees with you, her body language should match or be congruent. If her words and gestures are incongruent, you have reason to question her sincerity. As the ancient Chinese proverb goes, "Watch out for the man whose stomach doesn't move when he laughs."

Next, put together what you've captured from the 3 Cs of observation – **context**, **clusters**, and **congruence** – and reflect the speaker's underlying emotion in a paraphrase.

Empathizing might sound like this:

This is really worrying you, isn't it…
You sound very angry about how he handled it…
You seem disappointed with my analysis…

An amazing thing happens when you empathize with someone. The speaker actually experiences a catharsis: a softening in emotion, a sense of relaxation, and even acceptance. Generating such a response is certainly a powerful tool from a leadership perspective, but it is also a meaningful gift from a personal perspective.

Your act of empathizing readies a speaker to hear another view or perspective, one of which may very well be yours. It may also ready the speaker to move into problem solving mode or create a space where she is open to hearing advice.

MONITOR YOUR BALANCE

Together, the *Three Ways to Talk While You Listen* – questioning, paraphrasing, and empathizing – make up acknowledgement, or respectful listening. Some people think if they spend too much time acknowledging the viewpoints of others, it suggests they are agreeing or conceding. In fact, just the opposite is true.

Fully listening – in other words, hearing, understanding, and conveying your understanding of both the meaning and emotion of what is being communicated – allows you to more effectively advocate for your own ideas and position. It enables you to be more influential. That is leadership.

Think of every conversation as a balance between advocacy and acknowledgement. Advocacy is sharing your story or position, advising, or problem solving. When you advocate, you're doing most of the talking. You're dictating the direction of the conversation. Some conversations will demand more advocacy, some less.

We have a fallacious notion that successful executives push their ideas forward at any cost, and that this strength of will is what makes them leaders. Not true. The most effective leaders spend more time acknowledging than they do advocating. The most sustainable leader is one who listens and gathers as much input as possible before advocating for an idea, promoting a certain direction, or campaigning for a particular strategy.

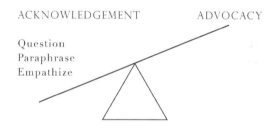

Starting today, I recommend that you begin monitoring the balance you're striking between advocacy (putting forward your ideas and opinions) and acknowledging (questioning, paraphrasing, empathizing). What's your ratio? If it's 90% advocacy and 10% acknowledgement, it's time to make a concerted effort to move the ratio to 80/20, and then to consciously strive for a ratio much closer to 60/40.

We've come a long way in our quest to listen like a leader, so let's revisit our sample conversation between you and your boss on the subject of the report you've written. Now it sounds more like this:

Boss: *I'd like to talk about the report.*

You: *Excellent. I'd love to hear your feedback.*

Boss: *Well, you got the basics down, but I don't think it completely hits the mark...*

You: *Mmmm.* (door opener)

Boss: *It has all the right sections and the organization is there, but the analysis doesn't cut it.*

You: *I'd love to better understand your view. Tell me a bit more.* (open-ended question)

Boss: *If we're pushing the idea of market expansion, we need the numbers that show growth in that arena.*

You: *If I'm hearing you correctly, you appreciate how I structured the report, but the analysis isn't convincing enough.* (paraphrase)

Boss: *That's an understatement! The analysis is missing in action!*

You: *You sound really frustrated.* (empathize)

Boss: *Yep, I am. I'm under a heck of a lot of pressure to get that report in on time.*

You: *Okay. So if I include a more comprehensive analysis of market growth to date, then our growth projections will better support our market expansion pitch. Correct?* (strategic question)

Boss: *Exactly!*

You: *Thank you for the feedback. I get it. I'll update the report with more robust market growth analysis. I'll also include a growth trajectory chart that I think would make the pitch more compelling. I'll have it for you by tomorrow morning.*

Boss: *Thanks. That would be great!*

This dialogue demonstrates precisely how listening with both ears, along with your eyes and even your mouth, will make you a valuable leader.

THE ELEVATOR WORKOUT

LISTEN LIKE A LEADER

I commit to power up my listening by:

_____ Delaying advocacy for my own position

_____ Questioning

_____ Paraphrasing

_____ Empathizing

To listen like a leader, I will:

Stop: _____

_____

_____

_____

Start: _____

_____

_____

_____

Continue: _____

_____

_____

_____

POWER PROFILE
$\mathcal{D}$OREEN $\mathcal{L}$ORENZO
President, frog

Fortune magazine considers Doreen Lorenzo one of the country's most powerful women.

She was commissioned by frog (no, that's not a typo) sixteen years ago to design one of their early websites. Not long thereafter, frog design hired her away from her previous employer with an eye on building their digital business, and neither she nor the company has ever looked back.

Doreen has now been with frog for fourteen years, and when she was the company's COO, she was instrumental in helping the firm grow from fifty people to 1,800. When KKR bought frog design five years ago, she was promoted to the position of President, serving dual roles as an Executive Vice-President and General Manager of Aricent, frog's parent group.

Over the years, Doreen has been influential in restructuring the company, taking it from a traditional design boutique to its position as one of the world's foremost global innovation firms, securing broad-based arrangements with an array of Fortune 500 clients.

Interestingly, Doreen's first pursuit was the theater. She says: "The beauty of the theater is that it requires a skill set for taking a creative concept and making it into something. Leadership in our field is not that different."

When Doreen arrived at frog, she saw a company heavy in both creativity and chaos. It was lacking infrastructure. Her task was to grow the business without losing its characteristic integrity and innovation. "I want to make our clients happy and our workers proud."

Her leadership philosophy is simple: Treat people the way you would want to be treated. Everyone wants to participate in a company's success. Everyone wants to feel a sense of ownership. Hire the best person for the job, and then let him or her do the job.

Doreen prides herself on listening like a leader. She understands that people want to be heard and acknowledged. "As a speaker, you have to know how to draw them in, hold their attention, and not beat them up with your message," she says. "As a listener, you have to show respect. You can't be answering phone calls or typing emails while they're talking. You block out time; you give the person sitting across from you your full attention."

While moving through the ranks at frog, Doreen has stayed consistently approachable. But she doesn't wait for people to come to her. She values casual encounters as well as more formal town-hall meetings, both of which require the same communication and listening skills. She goes out of her way to talk to her team and to allow them the freedom to give their input without having to agree with everything she says.

She also understands that it doesn't stop with listening. She will tell you that moving into action is just as important for a leader. "You have to act on what you've heard," Doreen explains, "or people will stop communicating just as fast as they stop caring. Make something happen, or people will cease to participate."

One of Doreen's favorite examples of listening and learning came when one of her teams suggested Summer Fridays. The idea was to reward a hard week's work by allowing people to leave at noon on Friday during the summer months. Doreen immediately saw the value in this and implemented the idea the following week.

Doreen takes the time to listen well, even to the most unconventional ideas. She takes them to heart. When the idea resonates, she follows up. When it doesn't, she is honest about it.

Doreen has a unique message for women who want to ride the glass elevator to the top:

"For one, you don't have to act like a man. Women approach leadership and problem-solving differently than men. Women have an incredible amount of compassion. Women compete in different ways than men. We believe in teamwork, and it comes naturally to us. Most of us have a nurturing side. Use what you have to care about your people."

PART TWO
CONNECT

THE GROUND FLOOR QUIZ
BUDDY UP WITH YOUR BOSS

My relationship with my boss is positive and productive.

____Never   ____Sometimes   ____Always

I know the best way to communicate with my boss.

____Never   ____Sometimes   ____Always

I understand my boss's expectations.

____Never   ____Sometimes   ____Always

I come prepared with agendas for meetings with my boss.

____Never   ____Sometimes   ____Always

I avoid badmouthing and find opportunities to compliment my boss.

____Never   ____Sometimes   ____Always

I seek out female role models or mentors.

____Never   ____Sometimes   ____Always

If you answered Never or Sometimes to even one of these questions, I invite you to continue reading and to be prepared to power up your relationship with your boss.

4

$\mathcal{B}$ UDDY UP WITH YOUR $\mathcal{B}$ OSS

Don't blame the boss. He has enough problems.

~ Donald Rumsfeld

- ▲ **Know thy boss**
- ▲ **Flex and forgive**
- ▲ **Invite yourself**
- ▲ **Be on the same page**
- ▲ **Say no nicely**
- ▲ **Ask for feedback**
- ▲ **Deliver your own review**
- ▲ **Buddy up with your boss's buddies**

There's something about bosses. They're not the most popular people in the world, are they?

Wherever my coaching work takes me, I hear people standing around gossiping and moaning about their bosses. Maintenance workers, cashiers, personal assistants, mid-level managers, executives; I hear it from all kinds. "My boss isn't quite right." "My boss isn't fair." "My boss has no people skills." And my favorite: "My boss is insane."

How is it possible for so many people to have bosses who are difficult, crazy, or toxic?

Women seem to think they have a corner on the "difficult boss" market. If the boss is male, you'll hear them whispering: "He's one of those alpha-males." If the boss is female, you'll hear them whispering,: "She's one of those alpha-females."

What is it about bosses? Is it something in their DNA? Something that happens biologically or psychologically when a man or woman takes on a leadership role or is suddenly thrust into a position of having to manage others? Probably not. But the fact is, studies show that the number one reason people quit their jobs is something directly related to … you guessed it … their boss.

A good number of people seem to paint bosses with the same broad brush they use for mothers-in-law. How is it that everyone seems to have a boss who is the biggest jerk on the planet or a mother-in-law who is a royal pain-in-the-you-know-what? Why do these two groups get such a bad rap? (On a side note, I'm one of the lucky ones. I happen to adore my mother-in-law, and, given that I run my own business, my boss ain't bad either!)

It goes without saying that there is nothing substantially different in the chemical or physical makeup of a boss. Statistically speaking, difficult or abusive bosses occur in society at the same rate as difficult or abusive people in general. However, I bet a disproportionate number of hands would go up if I asked everyone reading this book whether their bosses deserved the ubiquitous label of "difficult."

I can hear an echo now of people protesting, "But really, you haven't met *my* boss yet!"

Truth be told, few bosses are inherently evil (if yours, however, is truly abusive, I urge you to speak up). Yes, some are oblivious. Others are incompetent. Still others may be lazy. Some might shoulder a workload a bit larger than average, and some might be under a bit more pressure than others. But regardless of the perception you have of your boss, try to remember that she is a person just like you, and that she likely faces challenges and expectations you are not aware of.

Workplaces can be competitive environments. They are filled with diverse people with various styles and expectations. Mix them up in the corporate blender, push the "high speed" button, and step back – things have the potential to explode. For this reason, it can pose a particular challenge to forge productive relationships with every one of your colleagues. But if you learn to manage the relationship you have with your boss, as well as with other seniors, you will be well on your way to developing powerful Leadership Presence.

The term you often hear regarding the boss relationship is "managing up." But if you have your sights on an office upstairs, managing up is the simple part. While I will share with you solid strategies for doing this, we're going to explore something even more beneficial: how you can evolve into someone the workplace truly values and who makes her boss into an even better one. I call this "leading up."

KNOW THY BOSS

I have had more than one client turn to me and say unabashedly: "My boss is impossible to read. I have no idea what she wants!"

You have a choice in a situation like this. You can look at it as a "boss defect" or as a learning opportunity. If your goal is to ride to the top floor, my suggestion would be to seize the latter choice with gusto.

To build a successful relationship with your boss, you need to get to know her as well as you can. When I say "buddy up with your boss," I don't mean as a "drinking buddy." You may or may not choose to be friends outside the office, and she, of course, has the same choice. What I *am* talking about is being "professional buddies," those who depend on each other for mutual success, partners who jointly communicate, coordinate, and collaborate to produce great results.

Let's talk about some of the advantages of this positive relationship.

First, it will help you get a firm grasp on your new business situation and thus a jump on productivity and creativity. This fast start will help you avoid early mistakes that put you behind or expose you as less than competent. Second, the more positive this relationship is, the more likely you'll acquire the resources you need to facilitate your work. Third, a good relationship gives you a powerful leg-up on protecting your turf, an advantage not to be underestimated. Finally, you'll be in a position to influence others on your team from the get-go.

Whether you're starting a new job, moving into a new department, or accepting a position at the C-level, your first task out of the chute is to develop a productive working relationship with the person above you. Get to know her: how she thinks, what makes her tick, what she likes, and what she needs. Simply put, plan on initiating as many conversations with this very important person as you can. This is not kissing up; this is doing your homework.

If you're not new to your position, don't kick yourself if you feel you missed a few steps along the way in connecting with your boss or, worse, if you feel the relationship may be beyond repair. It's never too late to have a conversation. Good relationships are built one conversation at a time. And bad relationships get better one conversation at a time.

DIAGNOSE YOUR BOSS

Okay, so how do you begin this "buddy up with your boss" undertaking? By observing and learning.

Your style and hers may be as different as night and day; her preferences may surprise or annoy you. But challenging her on how she likes things done is a surefire way to put your working relationship behind the eight ball. For example, if your boss prefers to get settled into the day without interruptions and you barge in with two tall lattes in hand, ready to take on the world, don't expect her to do handsprings.

Start by getting a handle on how your boss likes to communicate. Is she taciturn or conversational? Is she laissez-faire or hands on? Does she like all the facts or just a summary? Don't guess. If it's early in your relationship, ask her point-blank. If you have a more established rapport, take some time to observe her preferences.

In any case, make it a point to know the answers to these questions:

- ▲ Does my boss prefer to communicate in person, via email, or by phone?
- ▲ Does my boss prefer scheduled or impromptu meetings?
- ▲ How often does my boss like to meet?
- ▲ When does my boss like me to be available? (First thing in the morning? Later in the day? 24/7?)
- ▲ How much information is TMI (too much information) for my boss?

▲ What types of decisions does my boss like me to consult her about before taking action?

▲ What types of decisions does my boss like me to make independently?

If these questions seem either rudimentary or unnecessary to you, picture how different the dynamics might be if you ignore them. And remember, you're not doing this just for your boss's sake. Leading up is about contributing optimally, garnering respect, and furthering your career.

FLEX AND FORGIVE

You don't have to like your boss's style or preferences. In many cases, those characteristics may strike you as ineffective, cumbersome, or just downright odd. But you must *understand* her style and *recognize* her preferences. And once you do that, your job is to learn to flex accordingly.

As a woman, you have the gift of empathy, an invaluable tool for flexing and forgiving. In Chapter 3, we loosely defined empathy as the ability to stand in another's shoes. Use this capability to influence your relationship with your boss. Understand that she is stressed with the task of delivering positive results to *her* boss. Be mindful of the demands that are made on her time, and appreciate that her successes are tied directly to the productivity and creativity of her team.

When you understand these things, you can flex and forgive. And once you're in this mindset, take an extra step and find out what makes your boss special – everyone possesses a bit of *wonderful*. Don't be afraid to share those discoveries with others.

The more different the two of you are, the harder you'll likely have to work at it. But the more effort you devote, the stronger your relationship will be. And once that connection between you is strengthened, the more likely you'll have her support or sponsorship when ascending the career ladder.

INVITE YOURSELF

To begin building this important professional relationship, make it a point to get on your boss's calendar on a regular basis at a set time. Is this once a day? Once a week? Figure out what you need time-wise to make an impression and fulfill your responsibilities, and use that as your baseline. If your boss isn't the one facilitating this regular calendar time, then take responsibility for making it happen without taking *no* for an answer.

Women often belittle themselves by saying: "Oh, my boss is too busy for me." This may seem like the case, but the truth is that your boss needs you; you're important to her. It's her responsibility to meet with you, to guide your work on behalf of the company, and to foster your professional growth. While it's part of her job requirement to offer this support, you may need to take the initiative to make it happen. Don't think you're being a nuisance or stepping on her toes. What you are doing is making your boss a better one by "leading up."

The thing to keep in mind when it comes to your scheduled meetings is to remember that this is *your* time. Invite yourself in with confidence – no peeking your head around the door with a sheepish apology for interrupting or shyly asking: "Is this a good time?" (If you need motivation, remember that the men in your office are marching in and demanding their time, assuming it is well deserved. You should too!) These regular meetings will cause the quality of your work to improve, which naturally shines a good light on her. This exchange is not simply quid pro quo; it is a mutually beneficial endeavor that will strengthen you both.

MEETING DOS AND DON'TS

When you have a meeting with your boss, always come with a well-prepared agenda. Be mindful, however, that it shouldn't contain a laundry list of every single thing you're doing. That's not an agenda; that's a surefire way to bore the pants off her and make her wonder about your organizational skills. The following checklist is a helpful framework for a successful meeting:

⬥ Strut your stuff into the meeting room.

⬥ Come prepared with 1-3 agenda topics.

⬥ Choose significant subjects that are relevant to your boss.

⬥ Use the magical CAR formula (from Chapter 1) to deliver updates.

⬥ Use the magical CQA formula (from Chapter 1) to communicate challenges. (Leave the list of problems back at your desk.)

⬥ Summarize your next steps at the meeting's end.

If you put all six of these bullet points into action during a meeting, I guarantee your Leadership Presence will be noted. You will be perceived by your boss as an employee who's a winner, not a whiner; as an up-and-coming leader who has gravitas; and best of all, as a partner who can help her get stuff done.

BE ON THE SAME PAGE

It's not a revelation that conflicts often arise when expectations are not clearly established. But for purposes of your success, it is up to you to take the lead here if your boss isn't going to.

Rest assured that any failure with regard to unspoken expectations will come to roost on your desk, not on your boss's. So whether your place in the organization is new or well established, get crystal clear on your boss's expectations. This goes for specific projects, to be sure, but it starts with her expectations in general. This pertains to everything, from issues as broad as work ethic right down to the time you clock in Monday morning. Leave no stone unturned.

For every project, clarify your boss's expectations at the outset regarding goals, timing, and measures of success, and be prepared to clarify and confirm these hot-button issues throughout a project. The questions you ask should be straightforward and pertinent to your situation or to the project you're working on. A productive way to achieve this is to express to your boss that you want to ask some questions to assure that you're both on the same page:

- ▲ What are your expectations?
- ▲ What is the timeframe?
- ▲ What are the milestones and what are the deadlines?
- ▲ When should I check in with you?
- ▲ What decisions can I make independently?
- ▲ Which decisions should I bring to you directly?
- ▲ What resources do you think I need?
- ▲ What will success look like from the company's point of view?

SAY NO NICELY

There are times when you need to say *N-O*. But let's not start there. Let's start with the secret to all good relationships: Say *yes* more often than you say *no.*

Check in with yourself: Can you safely say that your responses to your boss's requests and expectations are more often positive than negative? If not, then there is another problem at work, and you're going to have to ferret that one out first. But assuming you answered *yes* to my question, read on.

If your boss's expectations seem highly unfeasible, utterly impossible, or completely impractical, don't sweat it. Avoid a response of, "You want what?!" and refrain from stewing or badmouthing. The trick to master this is how you push back. Your best strategy will always be one that addresses what's important to your boss and the outcome she and the organization are looking for.

Use your Listen Like a Leader skills from Chapter 3 to fully understand where your boss is coming from and exactly what she wants. If you truly see what success looks like in your boss's eyes, you'll have a far easier time suggesting alternate routes for getting there.

First, take a deep breath and compose yourself. Then, take the opportunity to present yourself as a leader by sharing your own needs.

For example:

To maximize my contribution to this project, I'll need…

If you need more resources to accomplish one of your boss's requests, it is imperative that you accurately communicate how these added resources would help your boss achieve the results she wants. Similarly, if you're asking for some kind of schedule modification to the project you're involved in, make sure your boss understands how this will benefit the outcome of the project and how it will shine an even brighter light on the team.

When a request, demand, or directive is unreasonable, unfair, or, at worst, unethical, you may choose to say *no* or be forced to take a stand.

Is there such a thing as a nice *no*? How do you say *no* without destroying a valuable relationship, one that you are dependent upon in many ways? William Ury, well known for his popular book on negotiation, *Getting to Yes*, suggests an innovative framework that my clients use and love. It helps you deliver the *no* in a positive, productive, and powerful way. Ury calls this a "positive no."

The formula has three parts: **YES-NO-YES?**

Step 1: **YES**. Assert your *yes*.
Your *yes* communicates the needs, interests, or values that dictate your answer. It is your higher cause.

Step 2: **NO**. Communicate *no*.
While you may not even use the word *no*, you are respectfully communicating a *no* that protects the needs, interests, or values you articulated in Step 1.

Step 3: **YES?** Make a positive proposal for what you *will* do.
As you close one door, you open another in the form of a question.

Let's start with a simple, less work-oriented example to get our heads wrapped around this. Imagine a situation in which your young child is demanding a candy bar right before dinner and is doing so in the way only a child can (need I say more?). Instead of getting into a screaming match and driving your blood pressure through the roof, give the YES-NO-YES? formula a try.

(Yes.)   *It's important that we fill your little belly first with the kind of food that makes you grow healthy.*

(No.)   *After you have some dinner, you can have a candy bar.*

(Yes?)   *In fact, how would you like to pick out a candy bar right now and set it aside for dessert later?*

Now let's overlay this formula on a situation when your boss is demanding that you come in on a Saturday to finish a report.

(Yes.)   *I've made a commitment to coach my daughter's soccer team on Saturday.*

(No.)   *I want to find a time to perfect the report that doesn't conflict with my family commitments.*

(Yes?)   *What if I stay late on Friday or come in Sunday evening to make sure we meet the deadline?*

Nicely done. You've said *no* without upsetting the apple cart, and you've probably won some points in doing it nicely.

ASK FOR FEEDBACK

One mark of a good manager or boss is generous feedback. It serves to reinforce the things you do well and it also provides the opportunity for learning and growing.

The problem is that not all bosses are created equal when it comes to feedback. Some are generous with timely, specific praise. Some focus on the negative. Others offer none at all. In your quest to buddy up with your boss and mutually support each other's professional objectives, it is up to you. Be proactive in the pursuit of feedback.

How? Simple. Just ask! Here are a few examples:

What are your thoughts on how the meeting went?
Can you give me some feedback on my presentation?
I'd really like your impression of the product design so far.

But in asking, don't expect every ounce of feedback you get to be positive. Even critical or negative feedback presents an opportunity. You can either shrug it off, or you can use it to better yourself and your situation. Start by keeping an open mind about what you've heard. Ask for specifics. Accept the criticism you hear as readily as you would encouragement and ask: *What can I learn from this feedback? How can I improve?*

There's nothing wrong with our innate desire for some words of praise. Who doesn't like hearing her boss say: "Great job. Well done." In fact, you've probably noticed just how energized most of us get when we're on the receiving end of some positive feedback. It stokes our productive and creative fire.

I know one thing. You don't light a woman's fire with harsh words, biting sarcasm, or curt remarks. This is not to say that women don't respond well to constructive criticism, because we do. The operative word here is "constructive."

Timely, constructive feedback is like priming a pump. Hearing what needs improvement gives us something we can focus on with eagerness. It tells us what to continue doing and what to do more of to facilitate the best possible outcome.

If your boss gives you the amorphous "Great job!" variety of feedback, don't be afraid to dig for more. Let's say you've just made a presentation in front of a group of potential clients who responded with enthusiasm. Your boss pulls you aside and says, "Nice work." Don't be afraid to say:

> *Thank you. I'd love to know which parts you found most effective. That way, I'll be sure to include them in the next presentation. Of course, I'd also love to know what I could improve for the next go-round.*

This does two things. It tells your boss her feedback is important to you. It also gets you some face-to-face time with a person in a position to influence the upward direction of your career.

DELIVER YOUR OWN PERFORMANCE REVIEW

As you know, most companies have some type of formal performance review to let employees know how their work stacks up in the eyes of the people who count most. Some companies do it annually. Others do it more frequently. The bottom line in this process is the degree to which objectives and expectations have been reached. This review, whether positive or negative, should be looked at as another source of feedback, or information you can use advantageously.

It's a boss's job to deliver such a review as a means of rewarding and motivating you. Okay, I can already hear a few of you muttering sarcastically: "Yeah, right." I can see several others shaking their heads and saying: "I would be lucky to even *get* a performance review! Not in this lifetime."

As true as both of these statements might be, a woman can't sit back and let the chips fall where they may, not if she wants to get ahead in the workplace. You have to make it happen. If a review is not forthcoming, then ask for it. Schedule it yourself. And once it's scheduled, don't just show up. Come prepared. Arrive as if you're going to deliver the review yourself. You do this by walking into your boss's office with three invaluable pieces of information so well prepared that she can't ignore them:

- Top achievements for this period, with specifics and examples to back them up
- Areas you plan on developing in the period to come
- Resources and support you will need to develop those areas successfully

Whether or not your boss is prepared for such a review or proficient in the art of feedback, be prepared and skilled yourself. Take an active role in communicating your success; don't sit around pining for praise. Be as detailed as you possibly can about opportunities for professional growth. Take initiative and be your own best advocate. If you do, you're definitely a candidate on the fast track upward!

BUDDY UP WITH YOUR BOSS'S BUDDIES

Beyond the relationship you have with your boss, there are other critical relationships that you have to lead, not manage. Leading up is about making a contribution in the workplace that those around you truly value and communicating it.

Naturally, your boss is going to develop her most important opinions about you through personal interaction and on-the-job observation. But don't think that's her only source of knowledge.

Information, opinions, and perspectives reach your boss through any number of other channels, from the people below you on the corporate ramp to the people above you. Your boss's peers interact with you, observe you, and then, like most people, do what comes naturally to them: they talk. And guess whom they'll talk to? Yep, you got it.

You want to make a good impression, and the best way to do this is by being yourself, tried and true. Don't ever do anything disingenuous or inauthentic as a means of ingratiating yourself to anyone, much less your boss's buddies. It will backfire every time.

Instead, take care to identify with certainty the workplace players most connected with your boss. After you do this, get to know them. You can accomplish this most seamlessly through the projects that bring you together, but you should also make a point of reaching out to them. When you do encounter them, bring the best version of yourself to every interaction. That way, you'll never have to worry about who's saying what to your boss. And finally, never, ever badmouth your boss in the workplace. It's counterproductive to your ascent to the corner office where you'll one day be the boss (and when this chapter of the book will be about buddying up with you!).

BUDDY UP WITH BROADS

There can be volumes written about whether you're more or less fortunate to have a female boss or a male one, but there is absolute agreement – and less controversy – about our need for mentorship (and sponsorship, a subject we'll address in Chapter 6). A good mentor will offer advice tailored specifically to you and your situation. And it may very well happen that your mentor will be instrumental as a guide during the elevator ride. There is no set rule about whether your boss will also act as your mentor. It may happen, but it's just as likely that it won't.

Mentorship generally happens when you develop a natural, professional chemistry with a senior – male or female – in the workplace. In an effective mentor-mentee relationship, you and your mentor will get to know each other in a meaningful way and a relationship of trust will develop between you. You begin to share the good, the bad, and the ugly with them. Advice, connection, and opportunity ensue. All good things.

But if your boss ain't a "broad" and your boss's buddies aren't either, I urge you to also buddy up with as many women professionals as you can. Seek them out. Connect with them. Get their perspective. Women are great at offering friendship, nurture, and support. If they've been in the trenches, they can offer some critical rules of the game. Most important, they can serve as terrific role models. And frankly, they can be a whole lot of fun to bond with.

If your company is short on senior women, join an industry group, professional organization, or committee specifically directed toward women. 85 Broads (http://85broads.com) is a great place to start. If your geographic area doesn't have a chapter, why not start one?

Not too long ago, I was at a workshop where the professor heading the session asked the audience to call out the names of some great leaders. A squall of male names, generated by men and women alike, filled the room. Calls of *Gandhi*, *Churchill*, and *Clinton* (as in Bill) filled the air as did *Jobs*, *Gates*, and *Buffett*.

When we think of great leaders, often a host of male names come to mind. Why is that?

Historically, the most visible and recognized leaders have been predominantly male. There's no denying it. There's a bit of mythology associated with the great male leader, but, of course, men themselves have largely created it.

Don't be fooled. I'm here to remind you that there's a host of exceptional female bosses and leaders out there in the world and more coming on the scene every day. There's a very good chance that there are one or more in your workplace. I can guarantee that there are definitely extraordinary women leaders in your larger network.

It's time to discover them and call out their names. There's a wealth of knowledge to learn from them and so much to be gained. So seek out a powerful broad and buddy up with her.

Lead up.

THE ELEVATOR WORKOUT
BUDDY UP WITH YOUR BOSS

I commit to power up my senior relationships by:

_____ Learning more about my boss's style and expectations
_____ Preparing brief agendas for meetings
_____ Asking for feedback
_____ Connecting with women leaders

To buddy up with my boss, I will:

Stop: _____
_____
_____
_____

Start: _____
_____
_____
_____

Continue: _____
_____
_____
_____

POWER PROFILE

$\mathscr{L}$ISA $\mathscr{H}$SIA

EVP Digital Media, Bravo
NBC Universal

When the President of Bravo said to Lisa Hsia in 2005, "You're going to run Bravo Digital," Lisa didn't know a thing about digital. If someone had asked her what an SMS message was, she wouldn't have been able to tell them.

At the time, Lisa was at a place in her career where she could have played it safe. She was the Vice-President of *NBC News* and was flourishing. "Safe," however, is not how Lisa operates, and she jumped at the opportunity. Today, she oversees all of Bravo's extraordinary suite of digital assets, from the website, wireless, and apps to interactive television, gaming, and multi-platform programming. She has been instrumental in creating an interactive powerhouse, with a list of innovations that include the Infoframe, Bravo Talk Bubble, and Bravo Now.

Lisa's background makes her rise in the entertainment business even more fascinating. She grew up in Illinois, a first generation Chinese American. She likes to refer to her mother as a bit of a "Tiger Mom," a woman who impressed upon Lisa and her three siblings a culture of high performance. All attended Harvard, although school didn't come as easily to Lisa as one might assume. "It seemed like I always had to work twice as hard as everyone else," she says.

She took an unconventional route at Harvard, studying photography and documentary filmmaking. Her love of filmmaking paid off, and she took her talents to China when the country first opened up to Americans. An expertise in framing the unique world inside China's borders led to an offer from ABC's *Prime Time* during the Tiananmen Square uprising. Lisa thrived there and eventually became Diane Sawyer's producer. When she wasn't traveling the world, she shared a tiny office with a colleague who, years later, became the President of *NBC News* and hired Lisa as his lieutenant, where she oversaw *Today*, *Dateline NBC*, and NBC News Productions.

As impressive as Lisa's rise in the world of journalism may be, her approach to the workplace underscores why she is so successful. Lisa has always been a natural networker. She says: "I'm outgoing, so it was easy to put myself out there." Yes, it's about building connections, Lisa will tell you. But it's also about building deep friendships and dynamic, amicable partnerships with everyone at all levels of your organization. "From the furniture movers to the CEO," as she puts it. So while pleasing your boss is important, she says, you're also building relationships with people at all levels and across departments.

"Treating people with respect makes you a better person, a better manager, and it goes a long way in helping your business," Lisa explains. "It's also important to remember that every boss is different. You have to evaluate every relationship, and you have to use your emotional IQ to adapt yourself accordingly."

When Lisa took over Bravo's Digital Media department, she traded her waist-long black hair for a short, manageable cut, a symbolic gesture meant to give her a new identity as she embraced the challenge facing her. She was building the department from scratch and learning a new business on the fly. "You never stop learning. It doesn't matter how high up you go. The minute you stop learning is the minute you become a liability."

Recognized as a visionary in her field, Lisa has focused on driving innovation. These days, Bravo continues to be an engine for growth and change under the large NBC umbrella, and the conglomerate of digital businesses that Lisa has created is on the cutting edge of this movement.

Despite her success, there is nothing calculating about Lisa's leadership style. She doesn't think about "managing up" consciously. She strives to inspire those around her by having a vision and doing her job well. She focuses on bringing people together and building a team capable of maximizing good times and navigating tough times.

"My job is to get people to buy into what I'm doing. I know that the way to make things happen is to get everyone on board," she says. "I suppose it helps that I like people. I like to talk to them about their lives. I like to get to know them as people. And I like to mentor."

Lisa's message for women who want to take a ride in the glass elevator: "Be resilient. No matter what you do, you will hit obstacles, so you have to have the grit to succeed. You have to have the passion," she says. "Always keep your momentum going forward. Be tenacious and always give your best. What is the worst thing that can happen? You fail. It happens to us all. When it does, you get back up and begin again."

THE GROUND FLOOR QUIZ
TANGO WITH YOUR TEAM

I have high expectations of my team members.

____Never   ____Sometimes   ____Always

I delegate responsibility with an eye on what each person needs to grow.

____Never   ____Sometimes   ____Always

I hold regularly scheduled, productive meetings with my team members.

____Never   ____Sometimes   ____Always

I am generous with positive feedback.

____Never   ____Sometimes   ____Always

I deliver constructive feedback in an assertive and respectful way.

____Never   ____Sometimes   ____Always

I have fun with my team.

____Never   ____Sometimes   ____Always

If you answered Never or Sometimes to even one of these questions, I invite you to continue reading and to be prepared to power up your team.

5

*T*ANGO WITH YOUR *T*EAM

We don't accomplish anything in this world alone.

~ Sandra Day O'Connor

- ▲ Make the right partner
- ▲ Get close
- ▲ Loosen your grip
- ▲ Promote the positive
- ▲ Do the 3-Step
- ▲ Calendar consciously
- ▲ Celebrate to motivate

Various styles of tango abound, from the classic *Dancing with the Stars* varieties – the Argentine and the American – to the lesser known Canyengue and Uruguayan. Any number of techniques may be brought into play: close embrace, open embrace; small steps, long steps; heel leads, head snaps. But whether you prefer *Nuevo, Show,* or *Liso*, there are three things consistent in every tango: it's beautiful; it demands a strong leader; and, it takes two.

To make the dance beautiful, a strong leader has to be insightful and sensitive toward his partner. Being an effective team leader in the workplace – whether you're a manager, supervisor, department head, or C-level executive – is very much like taking the lead in the tango. Ken Blanchard, the highly recognized management expert, says: "In the past, a leader was a boss. Today's leaders must be partners with their people."

A good leader is often intelligent and magnetic. She is very likely skilled at planning, budgeting, and organizing, but there is more to leadership than those abilities alone. A strong leader knows how to get the most out of good people. She knows how to establish direction, inspire and empower, flex and collaborate – all of which are the makings of an inspiring tango.

Effective leadership and the tango have a number of other qualities in common. Neither is about pushing or shoving, pulling or prodding. (Talk about turning your partner off!) Both, however, are about finding balance, giving and taking, and connecting. In the tango, the chemistry between a leader and follower shows with every move. When purpose, motivation, and direction are clearly communicated in the workplace – when people and their ideas are respected and ownership is shared – the leadership dance is equally electric.

MAKE THE RIGHT PARTNER

Jim Collins, author of the best-selling book *From Good to Great*, likes to say that the greatest CEOs start by getting the right people on the bus and then determining what they're going to do. "First *who*, then *what*," is his famous catchphrase.

Catchy to be sure, but perhaps ideal. Let's be real. How many of us truly get to choose the men or women we're managing? Most of us step into situations already populated by good and bad players and have to make the most of it. *If only I could choose my own people*, you think, *I wouldn't have all these problems.* If you haven't said that to yourself, then you've probably heard someone else mouthing a similar complaint. Sure, I could write a book entirely devoted to the art of recruiting great talent. Instead, let's focus on making your people – the direct reports you have at this very moment – into the *right* people.

I'll begin by challenging you with this question: Is it possible that if you expected more from your team, you'd get more? Before you answer, let's visit a research study conducted in 1968 that tested the possible correlation between teacher expectations and student achievement. The study, conducted by Rosenthal and Jacobson, centered on an intelligence test given to California elementary school students at the beginning of the school year. The researchers randomly selected 20% of the students and alerted their respective teachers that these children were showing "unusual potential for intellectual growth" and that the teachers could expect a measurable learning spurt by the year's end.

Eight months later, they retested the entire student body. Across the board, the randomly selected group showed a significantly greater increase in test results than the children who had not been singled out. The teachers of these chosen students also rated them as more intellectually curious and happier than others. The conclusion was that a change in teacher expectations of these students actually led to the increase in their intellectual performance.

So what does this mean to us? It means you don't need to *choose* the right partner; you can *make* the right partner. Changing your workplace expectations can tangibly affect the performance of your team members. Perhaps Jim Collins was right after all when he said, "First *who*, then *what*." However, the *who* in my opinion, is *you*!

Start by taking a hard look at yourself and examining your expectations. Are you settling for mediocrity? Are you demonstrating a high level of confidence in team members' abilities? Are you taking direct action to unleash talent?

Next, look at your staff. Review your expectations of each of them as individuals. Be honest with yourself. Have you lost faith in anyone? Have you flat out given up hope on one of them? Is there someone on your team with potential and in need of more attention from you? It's time to raise your expectations. Give your direct reports the same type of psychological boost that the kids in our example thrived on.

There is an old saying from Ralph Charell: "Nobody succeeds beyond his or her wildest expectations unless he or she begins with some wild expectations." The great thing is, *you* can be the one to set them.

GET CLOSE

You've heard the expression, "Don't take it personally." Strike it from your vocabulary. *Everything* in the workplace is personal and women know it. They understand that people don't (or can't) check their emotions at the door when they come to work. Women managers know intuitively that a whole person enters the workplace, emotional baggage and all.

Recent studies by McKinsey & Company, a global consulting firm, have highlighted that the greater the number of women on an executive team and board, the better the company's financial performance. Why is that? While many reasons have been given for this unsurprising phenomenon, one hypothesis is that women use their understanding of how emotions play out at work to build valuable relationships. Their ability to get close to others at work lends to "empathic people development," which involves evaluating each person on their team personally and determining unique and effective ways to enrich that employee's experience.

I encourage you to embrace this natural tendency and put it to work. One of the best ways to figure out where the individuals on your team are coming from is to get to know them personally. What are their lives like outside of work? In what way could you show interest in their families or find out about their hobbies? Maybe one of your employees reads romance novels. Perhaps another belongs to a bowling league. What might this knowledge help you to understand about them? How could you use it to motivate them at the office?

As a leader, it's up to you to find ways to connect your team through non-work events during work hours as well as social events outside of work. Consider taking the team to a baseball game or to the symphony. If possible, have lunch catered in the office once a week. Institute a daily music break and let your staff choose the song. Get creative.

People work better (and enjoy work more) with people they like. And only by spending real time together and getting close do we discover how interesting and likable our co-workers really are.

LOOSEN YOUR GRIP

Ben Franklin famously said: "Tell me and I forget. Teach me and I remember. Involve me and I learn." A modern-day correlate for a manager might be: "Quit doing it all yourself."

Every senior executive at the C-level I know has faced and conquered the challenge of giving up total control, not only to help others mature professionally but also to allow herself to grow. When you fully involve others, you indeed give up a precious share of ownership. But you also free yourself up for the business of learning new things, taking on new responsibility, and moving up.

Micromanaging is out. Empowerment is in. By employing the following guidelines for loosening the grip, you'll be delighted at how fluid the leadership dance can feel.

ASK EMPOWERING QUESTIONS

I worked with a client who was so delighted about an opportunity to delegate more that she quickly drew up detailed instructions for every procedure – an exhaustive, by-the-minute playlist – so that her team members could take charge. When she proudly showed me the meticulous, multi-page Excel chart, I gently asked how her staff might feel when she shared it with them. She paused, made a funny face when the light bulb went on, and finally said: "Disempowered."

When we loosen our grip, we want to make sure our partners feel liberated. Consider involving your team members in pinpointing what they want to do, when they want to do it, and with whom they want to do it. Start by asking each person you manage some simple empowering questions:

- ▲ What would you like to learn?
- ▲ Who might you want to team up with?
- ▲ What projects would you like to spearhead?

PICK THE RIGHT TASK

In jointly choosing the right task to delegate to your direct report, you're naturally going to focus on something that needs doing or that you know needs improvement. But for the employee, it must be in line with his or her current level of competence. Getting it right is admittedly tricky, because the task should feel neither like a slight nor a bite too big to chew. Depending on the person, the task may range from a lower-tier community-building activity to something as significant as bolstering customer service.

PROVIDE DIRECTION

At the front end of delegation, a leader must provide a lucid picture of the purpose of the task, the goal, and how it fits into the bigger picture. Offering autonomy doesn't mean sacrificing accountability. Be clear about your expectations. In providing direction, don't forget to ask yourself: What do I need so that I can sleep at night without worry? Your answer might include things like scheduled check-ins or written updates about progress. Make sure to communicate all of your requirements up front.

SUPPORT EACH PERSON UNIQUELY

You've heard the saying: "Different strokes for different folks." Each of your team members has a different level of confidence and competence. If someone's on a steep learning curve, you may have to assume a hands-on role, actively teaching, coaching, and supervising. On the other hand, if someone is highly competent, you'll be doing more hands-off facilitation. (Some of you might have a direct report that is highly confident but totally incompetent, or conversely, highly competent but lacking confidence!) The key is to assess each individual, so you can support her with the right dose of expert listening, resources, and feedback.

LET GO, BUT DON'T DISAPPEAR

Delegating doesn't mean deserting or going AWOL on your team. You must be around to offer support and to coach. You'll be occasionally reminding the team that a smooth path does not always lead to success, nor does a hard landing signal a failure. You may have to run interference and advocate, if called upon. And most important, you'll want to be present to applaud wildly from the wings.

RECOGNIZE AND REWARD

While we typically think of reward as something that comes at the end when a completed project is delivered perfectly wrapped up with a bow, there are many things to recognize and reward along the way. Take the time to be a leader who appreciates and acknowledges things like effort, learning, initiative, tolerating risk, and reaching milestones.

When you empower the individuals on your team, you infuse the workplace with energy. When you delegate, you discover new levels of competency and capability in others. The upside? You'll get the best of your team, they'll be happier, and you'll be freed up to work on matters that will catapult you upward.

PROMOTE THE POSITIVE

I have a confession. I love hearing good things about what I do and how I do it. I love hearing great feedback from my clients. I love getting compliments from my friends. I love hearing words of appreciation from my kids and husband.

And I'm guessing that you're not all that different. Positive feedback is like a happy pill. It energizes us. It makes us want to keep up the good work, and it inspires us to keep giving.

When my clients complain about their direct reports, I often ask: "What did she do well?" They easily reply: "Well, she was really good at..." To which I answer: "Did you let her know how much you appreciated it when she did that?" While I sometimes get silence at that point, more often I hear: "Oh yeah, I made sure to say, 'Good job!'"

While saying "Great job" or "Well done" has a positive ring, it's simply not enough. Take your feedback to the next level by truly promoting the positive. Share with your direct report exactly what was great about what she did. In doing so, you'll be letting her know how to continue growing and succeeding.

To power up your positive feedback, here are three simple, hard and fast rules of thumb:

- ▲ **Be timely.** When you see something wonderful, don't delay in acknowledging it.
- ▲ **Be specific.** What was it *exactly* that you appreciated or admired? Put it into words.
- ▲ **Share the impact.** Tell your team member how her positive behavior particularly impacted you or the business.

For example, you could say:

Great work on that presentation. You really connected with the audience. They were fully engaged at every moment and even felt comfortable sharing their internal dynamic with you. I think we have ourselves some new customers.

BAN THE BUT

Everyone from the rookie to the star, from the assistant to the chief, needs feedback from time to time.

Yet, as true as this may be, Marshall Goldsmith, a world authority in the leadership development field, suggests we ban the word *feedback* from the workplace and replace it instead with *feedforward*. In other words, we shouldn't focus on the past, something we can't change. Rather, we should concentrate on future opportunities by helping others achieve a positive change in their behavior, their productivity, and their relationships.

Although I agree with this in theory, the word *feedback* is so deeply embedded in the workplace lexicon that I have a more practical suggestion. I propose we ban the word *but*. Why? Because most of the feedback I hear has a *but* somewhere in it, and the *but* is never positive and rarely productive.

> *Your presentation was very good, but the data section was way too detailed.*
> *Your product design is innovative, but it's not totally practical.*
> *You have all the credentials for the next level, but you're still too young.*

What kind of feedback is that? I can pretty much assure you that what the recipient of this so-called feedback heard was the message that came after the *but*:

> *You screwed up.*
> *You're impractical.*
> *You're too young.*

In fact, we're so programmed with this model of feedback that we often cease to hear anything with regard to the good points of our presentation, innovation, or great credentials. We're programmed for the hammer to fall. Why hear the good news, when you know the bad is right around the corner?

The solution is simple. Ban the *but* from your feedback repertoire. Or, at minimum, separate your thoughts about what was good and what leaves room for improvement with a big juicy period.

> *Your presentation was well structured and totally engaging. Nice!*
> (Period. Maybe even a pause.) *In terms of suggestions for the next run, I'd love to see a version with a shorter data section.*

GET POSITIVELY RADICAL

Not only am I going to suggest that you get more specific with your positive feedback and ban the *but* from any reactive conversation, but I'm also going to suggest something radical.

How radical? Well, if this is the one and only change you make in your management style after reading this book, I'll be jumping up and down. It's radical because so few people do it and because it completely transforms people. On top of that, it's easy to do.

On occasion, deliver *only* positive feedback. In a scheduled meeting or in a cubicle drop-by, share feedback that is 100% positive. Period. No negatives, no suggestions, no opportunities to leverage. It might sound like this:

> *I want to congratulate you on an excellent presentation this morning. You hit all of the client's concerns. You backed up all your ideas convincingly with data. You made it visually interesting with a mix of graphics and text. To top it off, you were funny, which made the whole thing even more engaging. The client was wowed. And so was I!*

As your team member raises her eyebrows waiting for the ubiquitous *but*, just say:

> *That's it. Just wanted to share that with you.*

I'll bet you a bundle that when you're out of the room, the employee will be on the phone gleefully sharing your feedback with a friend or a colleague. And I'll bet you another stack that same employee will be even more expert at whatever task lands on her desk the next go-round.

Here is what I recommend to push your team to the next level of productivity and creativity: Schedule regular "positively radical" sessions with every one of your direct reports. And please email me (really) at ora@oracoaching.com to share the amazing impact you experience from these sessions.

DO THE 3-STEP

No one enjoys conflict. Well, there may be the oddball exception, but not many. I think it's also safe to say that women in particular seem to hate conflict.

I'm not talking about "constructive" conflict, the kind that multiplies alternatives and helps us optimize high-stake decisions. I'm talking about "interpersonal" conflict, which takes a personal turn and can get uncomfortable and sometimes ugly.

In the face of extreme personal threat or conflict, there are two well-documented reactions: fight or flight. Generally speaking, men tend to favor the fight, or, in other words, the aggressive reaction. Fists come up, metaphorically if not literally. Women, on the other hand, generally favor the flight response, or the passive reaction. We run for our dear lives. But that, let me emphasize, is only in the face of extreme personal conflict. I'm praying the "extreme" does not exist in your workplace.

Nonetheless, when there's more than one human around, differences exist on many levels and conflict is often unavoidable. These are the kinds of situations that women are more likely to avoid than confront.

In the face of workplace conflict, women oftentimes replace the flight response with what is called a passive-aggressive response. We are passive in that we resist dealing with the matter at hand directly. Instead, we get aggressive when the person in question is *not* around, spending a lot of time talking behind the intended target's back with our best buddy. Too often it turns into gossip. Sometimes it turns nasty.

Let's be realistic. Responding to difficult situations in the workplace is an ongoing challenge. While fight and flight are not optimal reactions to difficult situations, neither is the passive-aggressive alternative. Thank goodness there's a third option: being assertive.

When we're assertive, we enrich and strengthen our working relationships, engage the people we manage in a dialogue, ease tension, prevent blowups, and help others change their behavior. Knowing when and how to give assertive feedback makes you a treasured leader.

There's a formula to help us deliver respectful feedback that has a positive impact. It's called the 3-Step Assertive Message.

THE 3-STEP ASSERTIVE MESSAGE

STEP 1	*When you...*
STEP 2	*I feel...*
STEP 3	*Because...*

Step 1: *When you…*

When your objective is to get an individual to change a certain behavior, describe the behavior in non-judgmental terms. The more specific and objective you can be, the better. Take evaluative terms out of the equation so no one can get defensive. Granted, this can be tricky, especially when you're upset.

If your goal, for instance, is to curb someone's habit of cutting off others in conversation, keep in mind that even a word like "interrupt" can have a negative connotation. Find a neutral or non-judgmental way to describe a behavior. For example:

> *When you start talking before I've completed my sentence…*

Step 2: *I feel…*

Now describe how this particular behavior makes you feel: Concerned? Worried? Disappointed? Angry? Whatever you feel, own up to your reactions. When you're authentic here, no one can argue with how you feel.

> *When you start talking before I've completed my sentence, I feel frustrated...*

Step 3: *Because…*

Explain the tangible, work-related impact, or more precisely, what effect that behavior has. Put all three steps together and it might sound like this:

> *When you start talking before I've completed my sentence, I feel frustrated because the newer members of the team don't get to hear all the steps they need to complete the process.*

In another context, it might sound something like this:

When you missed the client meeting this morning, I was upset because reliability will be a big factor in their final decision.

There's no yelling and no lashing out at the person. Instead, there is an assertive message about behavior delivered in a respectful tone.

From there, the most collaborative, straightforward segue would be a simple: "Let's talk about what happened." At this point your Listen Like a Leader skills from Chapter 3 will come in quite handy.

A more authoritative segue from your original 3-step message can be used when your goal is to give direction or provide a solution right up front, as in: "I'd like you to call the client to apologize and reschedule."

The 3-Step Assertive Message can be awkward at first. Don't be dissuaded. The more you play with it, the more you inject your own style and become more comfortable. You might consider experimenting with it at home. Try it on your kids or with your partner. Heck, try it on your mother. Believe me, it will work wonders there too. The kids' version might sound something like this:

When you leave your toys on the kitchen floor, I get worried, because someone can trip on them and get hurt. I'd like you take your toys to the toy box now.

Trust me, this works a lot better than screaming, HOW MANY TIMES HAVE I TOLD YOU NOT TO LEAVE YOUR TOYS ON THE KITCHEN FLOOR? First of all, it's more pleasant. And second, it's more respectful. And when people of any age are respected, they tend to respond in kind.

And guess what else? The 3-Step Assertive Message is so magical you can also use it to power up your positive feedback, making it specific and building in favorable impact. Try this on for size:

You delivered a well-structured, compelling, and funny presentation to the client. I was so thrilled. They loved it, and they're considering us seriously for the next project.

Do the 3-Step and be assertive in these situations:

- ▲ When you want to address something that's bothering you
- ▲ When you want to reinforce positive behavior
- ▲ When you value the relationship in question
- ▲ When you want to be respected as a leader on your way to the top

CALENDAR CONSCIOUSLY

Every leader worth her salt knows that communication is essential to relationship building and to an efficient workplace. Managers understand that it's important to have set meetings with their direct reports and team. So why is it not happening in the workplace with more regularity?

I know how often these meetings fail to occur because my clients tell me. When I ask about it, I get a lot of hemming and hawing: "Well, the meetings are supposed to happen, but half the time they get cancelled because of everyone's crazy schedule."

Then I get the ubiquitous rationalization: "And besides, we never get to the important stuff in those meetings anyway because there's so much stuff and not enough time."

Part of my work as an Executive Coach is conducting a "360" for my client. This means I interview all the colleagues in my client's sphere to learn more about their perceptions. I often ask my client's direct reports this powerful question: "What's the one big thing that would make your boss a more effective leader?"

You would be amazed how often I hear from her team: "More time with me." You can imagine my client's defensive retort: "But I have an open door policy. They can come talk to me whenever they need to."

Managers love to brag about their open door policy. Well, get ready for my rant on that one: It doesn't work, period. Not for you, and not for your team members. It doesn't work for you because you end up multi-tasking. And contrary to popular opinion, when you're multi-tasking, you don't get much done! Your open door policy doesn't work for your team because, well, you're multi-tasking, remember? You're distracted, which means they're a distraction. Or, at the very least, they feel like one.

We women pride ourselves on our multi-tasking ability, a survival mechanism in our demanding world. There is some scientific evidence to support that women are better at multi-tasking than men. But the more conclusive data reveals that multi-taskers – men and women alike – actually have more trouble focusing and shutting out irrelevant information, causing them to experience more stress. Simply put, heavy multi-tasking makes our thinking fractured, causes us to lose focus, and decreases our productivity.

So if your destination is a top floor in this high-tech, breakneck-speed world, you're going to need to use two old-fashioned tools in your quest to balance your time appropriately and become a powerful leader: a calendar and an agenda.

THE CALENDAR

When we consciously calendar regular individual and team meetings, they are more likely to happen. In addition to scheduling these appointments, you may want to take it one step further by arranging your open-door hours. This is different from a 24/7 open door policy. This may be an hour a day, or a half-day per week. When you set your open-door hours, two things happen. First, you generously offer your team a safe, productive time to drop by to discuss the small stuff, straighten out tidbits, and talk informally. On the flip side, you suddenly have closed-door time that people respect, which is essential for getting your own work done.

If you work in a cubicle or an open space, no sweat. Provided your work culture allows, put a sign up that says, "Open for Talking 1-3 pm" or "Closed for Working 10-12 am." Or, simply communicate respectfully when you'll be available. The net result will be that you're getting more done while still supporting your team, and you'll be advancing your cause for an office with a real door.

One last tip: You can take your conscious calendaring to another level by blocking out times for things like thinking, writing, making phone calls, meeting with clients, and checking email. With that in mind, schedule your high-energy times with more brain-demanding work, and save your low-energy times for less mindful work like emails.

THE AGENDA

When we create agendas for meetings, they are less likely to be cancelled and more likely to be productive. The great thing is, you don't have to create them all yourself. Drafting an agenda is actually an empowering task to delegate to team members. Ask them to prepare the three most important topics they'd like to talk about in their meeting with you, and have them send it to you a day in advance. Also make it clear that in addition to their points of discussion, you will take the liberty of adding one topic of importance to you.

CELEBRATE TO MOTIVATE

Motivating your employees and keeping them engaged and excited will become increasingly critical as you become more senior in your organization.

I hear too many managers complain about how hard it is to motivate their teams in tough economic times when the money pot shrinks. Sure, we're motivated by money, and yes, monetary rewards are important, but there are other means of motivation that don't cost a dime. Your employees' sense of value in the workplace is a major one. It's a huge reason why offering positive feedback to your people is so critical. Delegation is a crucial means of adding to this feeling of value. Expanding someone's opportunity to develop mastery and to have autonomy works wonders.

But there's something else that motivates employees, and it can be implemented even in the toughest of economic times: It's the celebration of life. It's the fresh donuts and hot chocolate you bring in for your team on a snowy morning or the surprise shower you throw for your assistant. It's the day off you arrange for everyone to work together at a homeless shelter or the birthday cake you personalize with a funny decoration. It's the toast, if not the roast, you make at an offsite dinner.

Simply put, by taking the time to celebrate, have fun, and tango with your team, you'll shine as an inspiring leader.

THE ELEVATOR WORKOUT

TANGO WITH YOUR TEAM

I commit to power up my team by:

_____ Helping my team members grow

_____ Promoting the positive

_____ Delivering assertive feedback

_____ Scheduling and structuring meetings

_____ Celebrating with my team

To tango with my team, I will:

Stop: _____

Start: _____

Continue: _____

POWER PROFILE

$\mathcal{G}$RETCHEN $\mathcal{S}$HUGART

CEO, TheaterMania

When TheaterMania CEO Gretchen Shugart received an award from the Alliance of Resident Theatres last year, it represented more than just her work in aiding the creation of theater in New York. It recognized a profitable approach to business that values people and heartfelt communication.

TheaterMania is one of those rare businesses that combine several platforms into one thriving enterprise. The company owns and operates two separate, but related businesses. The first is TheaterMania.com, an editorial website that markets and promotes the performing arts to nearly a million consumers each month. The second is OvationTix.com, on-demand software used by hundreds of arts organizations nationwide to manage ticket sales, fundraising, marketing, and patron information.

The woman at the helm of this transformational operation began her rise to the top after moving to New York to study the violin and landing a temp job with an insurance company to make ends meet. Gretchen ended up graduating from New York University's Stern School of Business, spending eighteen years in the financial sector and starting an advisory firm before becoming CEO of TheaterMania. An indirect route to the corner office, some would say, but one that allowed Gretchen to perfect the art of "managing down" while "leading up," long before there was terminology that described the process.

Gretchen set out on her own during the dot.com years when every Tom, Dick, and Harry (yes, mostly males) thought they had the latest and greatest Internet idea. Gretchen started her own financial services practice during that tumultuous time, offering expert financial advice to fledgling entrepreneurs and start-up businesses. One of her clients turned out to be TheaterMania. At the time, the company was running out of its angel funding.

Most people saw a company dying a quick death, but Gretchen saw an opportunity, believing in the business premise behind TheaterMania. So while many of the people involved in the company were headed for the exit, Gretchen kept showing up at the office and offering her services. TheaterMania's investors also saw an opportunity. They saw a woman with the skill set to run a business successfully and offered Gretchen the position of CEO.

Gretchen brought the company back from the grave with the support of the founders and a few key investors. She used her considerable skills in the area of creative finance to settle the company's liabilities and to generate new streams of revenue. Building back up bit by bit, the company settled into its dual mission of providing technology and services to support commercial and non-profit arts organizations.

Ten years later and TheaterMania is on solid financial footing, employing 55 people. The company supports hundreds of arts organizations, manages tens of millions of dollars in ticket sales, and has built a database with over 650,000 email subscribers.

Gretchen will tell you that if you pay attention to the needs of the market, if you build your operation around great people, and if you provide exemplary service, everything else will follow. The formula is surprisingly simple: First class technology plus world class service equals strong sales.

Believing in hiring smart, Gretchen brings into the company young people who are in the early stages of their careers or sometimes right out of school. She looks for people with energy and drive, people who are thoughtful, intelligent, and respectful by nature. Simply put, they have to be likable and committed.

She has built a small, stable team, with many of her original young hires now strong managers themselves. Her people stay with her, and Gretchen's explanation is simple: "Every business is a people business. You need to get to know your people. You need to understand their perspective and what they want. This goes for your clients and your prospects, to be sure, but it also goes for your employees. They need to trust you and respect you. Every person is important to our mission, and I value everyone for what they do."

Gretchen sees herself as a leader and a manager but also as a team member. "I'm not perfect, but I try to talk to people at every level. I give them a voice. I give them a chance to speak and to be heard, and a chance to disagree. I solicit opinions. I encourage people to say what they think. I ask them to get to the point but to be diplomatic and kind while they're doing it."

Gretchen believes strongly in the use of feedback as a means of motivating her team. She calls assertive feedback a sign of respect. "I like to give it and receive it."

At TheaterMania, performance reviews are not tied to compensation. A performance review is an opportunity to hear what's on an employee's mind and to help him or her in the workplace. "I believe in laying everything on the table. A business is like a family. If a family doesn't face issues and talk, it becomes dysfunctional. A business must talk to be functional."

Gretchen's message for women who want to ride the glass elevator is: "Be curious. Speak up. Ask questions about the big picture and how your job fits into it, and you will naturally rise level to level. Push yourself to understand how things work. But most important, sparkle with interest."

THE GROUND FLOOR QUIZ
GROW YOUR TRIBE

I pursue relationships with a broad range of professionals.

____Never   ____Sometimes   ____Always

I take time to personally get to know the people with whom I work.

____Never   ____Sometimes   ____Always

I am generous with others at work.

____Never   ____Sometimes   ____Always

I take the time to connect people in my network.

____Never   ____Sometimes   ____Always

I attend industry events.

____Never   ____Sometimes   ____Always

I use social media.

____Never   ____Sometimes   ____Always

If you answered Never or Sometimes to even one of these questions, I invite you to continue reading and to be prepared to power up your tribe.

$\mathscr{G}$ROW YOUR $\mathscr{T}$RIBE

*Never doubt that a small group of thoughtful, committed people
can change the world. Indeed, it is the only thing that ever has.*

~ Margaret Mead

- ▲ Seek a sponsor
- ▲ Nurture six needs
- ▲ Be likable
- ▲ Give to gain
- ▲ Play with your peers
- ▲ Grow a third leg
- ▲ Get some fresh air
- ▲ Fuse technology and tribe

There's an ancient African saying: *It takes a village to raise a child.* No, this is not a chapter about child rearing, but rather one focused on giving you the best shot at advancement in the workplace. And like raising a child or anything significant in life, you can't go it alone; it really does "take a village." You need the support, inspiration, and influence of people both inside and outside your organization – your tribe.

Let's start with a few social networking questions. How many Facebook friends do you have? How many LinkedIn connections have you made? What about followers on Twitter? If your number is paltry compared to the hundreds or thousands that some networkers lay claim to, how does that make you feel? Embarrassed? Resigned? If you're one of those people with connections and followers in droves, are you proud of it?

The rise of social networks and the extraordinary hype that has accompanied them have put an emphasis on quantity. The number of friends, connections, or followers you have has fallaciously become the new measure of how impressive your network is. The subject of quality, however, is begging attention.

You may have heard of the man who wanted to test the quality of his social network, so he invited all of his Facebook friends, LinkedIn connections, and Twitter followers to meet him for a birthday celebration in a local bar one Friday evening. Guess what happened? Exactly one person showed up, and he didn't know her from Eve. That suggests a problem.

Networking is a popular word in the business world, but the word *network* tends to convey an image of something cold, distant, and not particularly accessible. A *tribe,* on the other hand, sounds warm and familial, supportive and influential. It's the kind of group that starts small and then grows modestly and meaningfully, involving more than a click of a mouse.

We've all heard the age-old adage: *It is not what you know, but whom you know*. Ask any executive about her rise to the top and you'll hear plenty of mention of the people who supported her along the way. That's no surprise. But I think our old adage needs some rejuvenation. It should read: *It is not whom you know, but how well you know them.*

We all need a tribe. A tribe teaches us new things and helps us do our jobs better. A tribe supports and energizes us. The power of *we* is a lot more commanding than the power of *me.*

Here's a fun yet illuminating example: A jar of jellybeans was placed in front of a renowned mathematician and her task was to guess the number of beans inside. The same jar made the rounds of a state fair, hundreds of people of all ages asked to make their own estimations. It turns out the average of the state fair crowd's guesses was more accurate than the single estimate of the mathematician. How is that?

Think about the television show, *Who Wants To Be A Millionaire?* If you've seen it, you're aware that when a show contestant doesn't know an answer to a particular question, "asking the audience" is often a successful choice, because empirically speaking, the collective opinion tends to yield the correct answer.

This same theory can be applied to our professional circle: Why go it alone? Whether you're building a dam, a jigsaw puzzle, or your own career, the support of many people gives you a boost. Everything takes a tribe, or more specifically, it takes the relationships that grow within it.

Before we discuss relationships, however, we must first acknowledge gender differences. While men tend to benefit from the *breadth* of their professional connections, women are more likely to create relationships with *depth* – those that are both sustainable and that sustain us. Both types are valuable; but in order to strike a productive balance between the two, as well as propel ourselves upward, we women must learn how to extend the breadth of our professional relationships without sacrificing depth.

One challenge women often face in expanding our tribes is that we're so busy helping other people that we don't ask the critical question:

Who can help me?

In a book about getting ahead in the workplace, you might think I'd suggest building a network dominated by power players. On the contrary. Diversity is the key to a successful tribe. If you look at the spectrum of top-ranking executives across industries nationwide, you will find men and women with diverse networks, illustrating that your tribe will best thrive when it is composed of various personalities who each offer a unique, high-quality relationship.

Connecting with people on all rungs of the corporate ladder – at work and outside – is equally important as you strive to build your own eclectic tribe. Colleagues and friends will help you get through tough days. Bosses can give you helpful feedback and unselfish guidance. Sponsors may go to bat for you. Women leaders often serve as your role models and become mentors. Clients offer you heartwarming validation. Peers in other functions can share best practices and solid counsel. Industry contacts can keep you updated on trends and research. Coaches can help you develop Leadership Presence. Family can keep you centered on your values.

So when it comes to building your tribe, choose up, down, and all around to ensure you're nurtured from every direction.

SEEK A SPONSOR

A 2010 report by Catalyst, a non-profit organization dedicated to expanding opportunities for women and business, had both inspiring and less-than-inspiring news to share.

The disheartening note of their report was the revelation that women's representation in corporate boardrooms and executive suites around the country had stalled after many years of trending upward. The more encouraging news was the effectiveness of *sponsorship* in reversing this trend.

Sponsors are people in more senior positions who advocate for your career-growth opportunities and promotion. They are, as Catalyst put it, the "silver bullet" in opening doors to the C-suite for women.

Historically, men have had an advantage when it comes to sponsorship. They have long benefited in terms of promotion and compensation by having strong senior sponsors. Not surprisingly, their sponsors are usually male.

Having someone influential in your tribe helps when it comes to advancement, but many women have been known to call this kind of pull in the workplace an unfair advantage. My response to that: Get over it! Seek a sponsor.

I'm sorry to say that hard work alone does not always get you where you want to be. A powerful voice trumpeting your cause helps. It not only helps with your advancement, but it also increases the scope of your own influence and persuasive power, something we'll discuss in the next chapter.

The problem is that women are only half as likely as their male peers to have a sponsor. We have to change the odds. Seeking sponsorship from a senior leader whom you admire and respect is a must. It begins with connecting, progresses to building a trusting relationship, and ends with asking. If asking is not your strong suit, remember that sponsors don't usually come to you.

You will discover that a sponsor is an exceptional asset when it comes to bolstering your confidence and improving your performance. With an active sponsor on board to push you, the percentage of women (and men) who will ask their bosses for career-boosting assignments or pay raises increases dramatically – a statistical career benefit of 22-30% according to the research. That is nothing to sneeze at.

The more you grow your tribe, the more potential sponsors you'll encounter. And once you have a sponsor alongside you in the elevator, you'll practically be flying upward.

NURTURE SIX NEEDS

When you're building your tribe, keep in mind you have six needs you'll want to nurture. They are:

1	Support
2	Expertise
3	Influence
4	Feedback
5	Validation
6	Energy

Research conducted by Rob Cross of the University of Virginia and Robert Thomas of Accenture Institute for High Performance suggests that your tribe will be infinitely stronger when you have two or three quality people, fulfilling each of these six needs. That's somewhere between twelve and eighteen people in an effective network. How hard is that?

With that in mind, grab a pen and fill in names to answer each of these need-related questions:

Support:

Who supports me personally at work?

_____

_____

_____

Expertise:

Who shares knowledge or expertise with me?

_____

_____

_____

Influence:

Who provides political support and influence on my behalf?

_____

_____

_____

Feedback:

Who provides feedback and watches out for my career development?

_____

_____

_____

Validation:

Who makes me feel good about my work?

_____

_____

_____

Energy:
Who helps me stay energized?

_____

_____

_____

If you see holes in your list, you now have some clues as to what kind of relationships you need to pursue. If you see an imbalance in support of your six needs, think about where you need to maximize your efforts going forward.

For most of us, when business is as usual, a warm, devoted tribe of twelve to eighteen members is sufficient to sustain us professionally and nourish us personally. But I don't want to discount the need for a larger tribe, albeit a less intimate one. A seismic change, such as losing a job, is one instance when you need to reach beyond your inner circle. Similarly, if your goals point in the direction of large volume sales or a strong media presence, expanding your social network to hundreds or even thousands of followers will be essential.

With a core of twelve to eighteen devotees in place, it's time to explore ways you can expand the breadth of your tribe.

BE LIKABLE

Being likable may sound too simplistic to consider, but it's the easiest way to strengthen your tribe. People like people who like them. It's human nature. Shakespeare's classic *Much Ado About Nothing* depicts a sample case: The main players, Beatrice and Benedick, fall madly in love only once they are tricked into believing that each one loves the other.

We all have a deep desire to be liked, accepted, and valued, and we end up liking (or loving) the people who ... yes ... make us feel liked, accepted, and valued. So, how can you be likable? Start by liking others.

Likability often comes from familiarity. You have to get to know people before you discover how much you like them. Start by asking yourself how much you really know about the people you work with every day. Do you take the time to stop and chat? It doesn't require much effort to ask someone about life outside of work. Where is she from? What does she do for fun? What about family? Start connecting over coffee or at the local watering hole.

Since people tend to like those who are similar to them, explore what you have in common. Are you both from, say, Ohio (like me!), or alums of, perhaps, the University of Pennsylvania? Are you both looking for quality schools in the city for your children? Do you both practice yoga? As you learn about each other's interests, you may uncover the kinds of wonderful things that lead to what I call "falling in like."

And one last thought regarding likability that we touched on in Chapter 2: *the halo effect*. Remember our tendency to assign additional positive traits to attractive people? Others will like you for all sorts of reasons when you look good and have a smile on your face. And when people like you, they will definitely want to join your tribe.

GIVE TO GAIN

Another way to grow your loving and loyal tribe is to be generous. When you give, you always gain. And I'm not just talking about the great feeling you get from being generous. A recent study by researcher Shawn Achor reported in *Harvard Business Review* shows that employees who scored highest on providing social support – helping others, inviting coworkers for coffee, and organizing office social activities – had significantly higher job satisfaction and were 40% more likely to receive a promotion in the following year.

If that's not sufficiently compelling, there's yet another benefit to giving generously in the workplace. When you give to someone else, she has an urge to reciprocate. When a friend invites you over to dinner, how long does it take you to start thinking about when you might invite her over in return?

We are inherently motivated to return favors, even unwanted ones. Sometimes repayments exceed the value of the original gift or favor. I can attest to that. A colleague of mine once made a quick but very valuable call for me, and I soon found myself in Bloomingdale's buying her a designer scarf to express my gratitude.

In order to gain from the power of reciprocation, we must be generous. When we give generously at work, we establish a cache of goodwill. Naturally, the more people we share with, the bigger our devoted tribal circle.

There are four fundamental ways we all can give generously at work: through **words**, **time**, **service**, and **gifts**.

Words

When you see, hear, or experience something nice, say something nice about it. Use words of affirmation, praise, and appreciation, and use them often.

Time

Spend time with people, and not just at your desk or in the cafeteria. The best way to forge relationships is by doing something enjoyable together. And it doesn't have to be golf. It can be breakfast or drinks after hours. It can be biking, billiards, or baking. It can be fifteen minutes or two hours. It all counts.

Service

Be of service by offering information and updates, taking on extra tasks if someone needs a break, or helping a new hire get up to speed. Extend your network to others. Become a coach, mentor, or advisor.

Gifts

Remember special days, and not just holidays. Consider a gift for birthdays, babies, moves, and promotions. Gifts need not be expensive. Cards and cupcakes make people just as happy as picture frames or coffee mugs.

Don't delay in being generous to grow your tribe. Start right now by choosing someone to help, and leverage your unique strengths as a woman. If you're a wonderful communicator or consensus builder, tap and share that skill. If you're a collaborator or connector, seek to extend that gift to someone.

Who can I help this week? Choose someone.

_____

How can I help? Don't over think it. Keep it simple and doable.

_____

_____

_____

_____

PLAY WITH YOUR PEERS

I've witnessed my fair share of workplace turf wars. In companies of all sizes and within every industry, I've seen battles fought over projects, positions, and people. When resources are tight within a business — and really, when aren't they? — there's going to be competition, and it can get ugly. Unfortunately, it's often peers who are competing for attention and resources.

The antidote for this challenge is to find a way to replace competition with collaboration and to make your peers members of your tribe. When you play nicely, best practices emerge. Economies of scale develop, clients are better served, and you personally have the help you need when you want it.

And there's another wise reason to play nicely with your peers: not all of them will remain at your level indefinitely. I guarantee you that one or more of your current peer group will end up on a promotion committee, as your boss, or even as your direct report. The bond you build now will ease your relationship later. If they are not yet "family," start by welcoming your peers into your tribe today.

GROW A THIRD LEG

You've undoubtedly experienced the power of three. A tricycle is more stable than a bicycle. Three phrases strung together is a haiku. Even your personality, according to psychoanalytic theory, is composed of three elements. Likewise, many memorable things come in threes. The Three Stooges. The Three Little Pigs. The Holy Trinity. The three-word Latin phrase *omne trium perfectum* tells us that everything that comes in threes is perfect.

So it's not surprising to hear authors Logan and King argue in their book *Tribal Leadership* that when two people connect with a third to create a triad, they form a far more stable and effective structure. Adding a third member to every twosome increases not only the size of your tribe, but also its stability and power.

Drawing upon research from a ten-year study of more than 24,000 people in two dozen organizations, the authors argue that tribes made out of triads have the greatest influence in determining how much and what quality work gets done. Therefore, if you're part of the tribe, you're part of the power. And what better support for women who want to move up in the workplace?

The trick is to add that third, well-chosen, and well-purposed player to each of your partnerships. Start by looking at the people who currently nurture your six needs with expertise, influence, support, feedback, validation, and energy. If you have a treasured connection with a person who always provides insightful feedback, for example, who might that person value knowing?

I have a colleague I adore named Shira. We are two peas in a pod when it comes to our energy and our interests. Some time back, Shira was looking for someone to collaborate with on an important project, and I had recently met Valia at a networking event. Valia exuded loveliness and smarts, and she seemed to be a perfect fit for Shira's needs. I introduced them and sure enough, they began working together, and the arrangement couldn't have been more productive and enjoyable. We're now three peas in a pod. But it doesn't stop there. My daughter, Noa, was looking at an internship opportunity at a company where Valia was once employed, so I introduced them, extending a third leg in a different direction. Now Ora-Valia-Noa is another effective triad.

In this day and age when everyone groans that there's no time for networking, cutting down on one-on-one meetings and focusing on trios makes networking more efficient and more fun. Your connections will be delighted to meet each other. After all, two's company, but three's a party!

GET SOME FRESH AIR

There is no doubt that your company is a wonderful place to broaden your sphere with seniors, peers, and juniors. Deepening these connections by taking them beyond the workplace and sharing your interests can be wonderful, but sometimes you need fresh air. In other words, you need to extend yourself beyond your company culture.

A great way to do this is by attending industry events and conferences. But let's get real for a moment. A lot of you are probably like me and suffer from Event Dread. Sometimes I can't bear the idea of walking into a room filled with strangers and mustering up the energy to introduce myself and make small talk. I'd rather go home, put on my sweats, and curl up on the couch with my iPad.

A couple of years ago, however, my network was feeling a bit stale and my tribe needed some rounding out. *How*, I asked myself, *can I conquer my Event Dread?* My answer: *Volunteer!* There may be no better way to seamlessly become part of a warm, welcoming tribe. Here's a prime example:

We have an excellent chapter of the HRPS (Human Resource People and Strategy) organization here in New York City that puts on monthly events, featuring speakers from companies with innovative leadership development practices. This is just the kind of stuff that I love. It's a great learning venue, and it's also a great place for me to connect with people in my professional realm. But when I considered the idea of mixing with a group of HR professionals gabbing over danish and coffee before a lecture, I came down with a bad case of Event Dread. I needed less intimidating access to fresh air.

I volunteered to become – get this – a "Door Greeter." Anyone can do this job! As a Door Greeter, I say hello, smile, and check names off the registration list. As it turns out, I'm now a familiar face to a good number of important connections. Over time, I became friendly with Kay and Paula, two terrific volunteers (and yes, we're a triad!), so much so that Kay provided me with some excellent feedback while I was writing this book, and Paula invited me to a stimulating lecture at her firm. All of this without having to stand around feeling awkward and eating breakfast danish I don't need.

Michelle Gloeckler, a Senior Vice-President at Walmart who's profiled at the end of Chapter 8, will tell you that volunteering has been a huge boost for her professional career. She urges everyone she mentors to join professional organizations and connect with people from other companies.

My personal footnote to Michelle's advice is to always follow up with the people you meet at these types of events. You can connect on LinkedIn or Facebook, or you can make it more personal by sending a simple email:

I so enjoyed meeting and talking with you yesterday. I look forward to connecting at our next event.

Over time, something surprising happens: Event Dread dissipates and is replaced by something totally invigorating. I call it "tribal fresh air."

FUSE TECHNOLOGY AND TRIBE

You might have heard the term *six degrees of separation*. Well, it's *six degrees* no longer. The average number of acquaintances separating anyone in the world is now 4.74. This lower number means that it is even easier to target almost anyone we'd like to connect with. We can credit technology for this new, shrinking world. In fact, your online presence has become as important to your professional ascent as your face-to-face connections. So why fight reality? Embrace it. Lucky for us, social media provides us with two indispensable benefits: **access** and **awareness**.

ACCESS

While it is true that the face-to-face connection with our primary tribe is what truly nourishes us, there are plenty of times when we need to be more broadly connected. In other words, we require more access.

Let's take the search for new employment as an example. Yes, the twelve to eighteen people who make up your primary tribe may be in a position to help, but they may not be able to unearth the kind of connections you need to score the job you want. Enter social media. Currently, 79% of US hiring managers and job recruiters search and review online information about job applicants, and 37 million people say they found their current job via social media.

Though broad social media connections are weaker than your primary tribe, they can be instrumental in enhancing your Leadership Presence by providing information, solutions, exposure, and partnerships you may have never considered, all with just a click of the mouse. Within various arenas, these connections are worth cultivating and can often prove vital to your growth and success.

AWARENESS

In addition to access, growing your tribe technologically gives you awareness. Staying connected with a broader professional tribe by blogging, posting, and commenting is one of the best ways I know to stay current with the goings-on in your field. What is less obvious, however, is that staying connected socially is a magnificent way of developing what has been coined *ambient awareness* of a large number of people. When someone updates her status with her Saturday morning trip to IKEA or posts a picture of her child's little league team, you become a bit more aware of what is going on in her world.

Taking a few minutes every day to skim and acknowledge posts is a way for us to deepen our knowledge of the members of our extended tribes. When we either need or choose to do so, we can use the bits of stored information to help us connect with them more meaningfully and naturally.

A colleague of mine named Walter Akana is both a coach and an online identity strategist with a passion for social media. Walter was the first person with whom I thought of connecting when I began writing this chapter, despite the fact that we had not seen each other in nearly a year.

Walter is closely connected with a digital tribal community that extends to all parts of the world through tools like Twitter, Pinterest, and Instagram. And, for the record, for those of you who think you're "too old for this," Walter is (forgive me, Walter!) no spring chicken.

He and I scheduled a phone chat. And the minute I heard his voice, I gushed, "Walter, I am so jealous of your workouts! Tell me more about them." In short, Walter is a workout nut. He regularly and enthusiastically posts updates about his boot camp workouts on Twitter and Facebook. Being a fellow fitness enthusiast, I had noticed his posts and was eager to hear about them, as are many of his friends and followers. Walter also posts pictures of his cats online, a surefire way to connect with other animal lovers.

"The goal is to stay on people's radar," Walter explains. "You can do this by interacting in small doses on a regular basis."

Often it is the little things that interest people – the articles you read, the music you listen to, and the places you visit. By fusing technology and tribe, you gain access to and awareness of others. At the same time, it creates broad ambient awareness of you.

With the rapid growth of social media, we have no choice but to embrace it to grow our tribes and advance professionally. Googling, blogging, texting, friending, and connecting have become second nature to millions of us. If your feet aren't yet wet, be brave and jump in.

Though it can be hard to keep up with the tools being invented and released every day, learning what's new can be part of the fun.

And remember: The same principles that apply to our in-person networking apply with equal force to social-media networking. Be likable. Be generous. Be respectful.

There is a direct correlation between growing your tribe and growing yourself. They go hand in hand.

Start by connecting with me!

Visit my site and subscribe to my vlog for video tips for success: http://oracoaching.com

"Like" my Facebook Page for posts on leadership: http://facebook.com/ORA.Executive.Coach

Connect with me on LinkedIn to broaden your tribe: http://linkedin.com/in/orashtull

Follow me on Twitter for titillating tidbits: http://twitter.com/coachora

Email me with personal questions or feedback: ora@oracoaching.com

THE ELEVATOR WORKOUT

GROW YOUR TRIBE

I commit to power up my tribe by:

_____   Inviting a colleague for coffee
_____   Being generous to someone at work
_____   Creating a triad in my network
_____   Attending an industry event
_____   Increasing my online presence

To grow my tribe, I will:

Stop: _____

_____

_____

_____

Start: _____

_____

_____

_____

Continue: _____

_____

_____

_____

POWER PROFILE
$\mathcal{N}$ICOLE $\mathcal{S}$ANDFORD

Partner
Deloitte & Touche LLP

Nicole Sandford joined Deloitte & Touche, one of the "big 4" accounting firms, after graduating from Niagara University. That was eighteen years ago. She has since traveled a circuitous route that finds her today as one of the leading authorities on corporate governance in the country.

Corporate governance, the process by which corporations are managed and controlled with responsibility and transparency, was hardly a hot-button issue in the early 1990s. Nicole, however, was as passionate about corporate responsibility and exceptional client services back then as she is today. She was also on the cutting edge of networking long before the term was in vogue.

"Nothing," Nicole will tell you, "replaces passion. If you're passionate about your work, you'll thrive. If you're only doing it for promotion or pay, your performance will reflect that."

While following her passions, Nicole also has a decidedly astute insight into the need for balance at home and in the workplace. "If it's not good personally," she says, "it won't be good professionally." Nicole knows from experience that achieving this elusive balance isn't easy. She was a single mother with two kids for many years while struggling to start up her practice in the corporate governance arena. Her third child arrived shortly before her current husband was deployed with the military in Afghanistan.

Nicole discovered a philosophy back then that she continues to employ every day, and which she readily shares with women in the workplace. She says: "There are always roadblocks and there are always hurdles. You can let them get in the way, or you can turn them into energy. And when you're feeling energized, work is fun."

When the Enron scandal occurred in 2001, it was a turning point for corporate governance, and, by either luck or foresight, Nicole was at the forefront of the movement. She founded the Deloitte Center for Corporate Governance, which has since become a major player in providing the latest research and information on leading governance issues for boards of directors nationwide.

Nicole also founded Deloitte's Diversifying the American Board program, which works to match board-ready executives from nontraditional backgrounds with corporate boards seeking diverse members. In 2008, she was named a "Rising Star of Corporate Governance" by the Millstein Center for Corporate Governance and Performance at Yale University's School of Management.

Now a sought-after speaker and well-respected author, Nicole has a message for women who want to soar professionally: "Every time I did something that may have looked on paper like a step backward – such as spending more time with my family or deciding to work from home – they were decisions that were good for me; and every time you make a decision that is good for you, it's a huge step forward no matter how it looks on paper."

She will also tell you that you can't make it alone in the business world. You need people. You need their input and their energy. You need to connect. You need to network. A self-proclaimed "networking queen," she'll tell you that an external network is just as important as an internal one.

A proponent of the original form of "social" networking, she believes a face-to-face lunch with absolutely no agenda can be the most valuable thing you'll do in a day. "There is no substitute for talking and listening with people, and you can't do that over the Internet."

She says: "I don't network to get something from people. Not consciously. I network because I'm interested in everything and everyone. And I know that my most valued collaborators are the ones who inevitably grow out of my ever-expanding circle."

PART THREE

INFLUENCE

THE GROUND FLOOR QUIZ
INCREASE YOUR INFLUENCE

I'm comfortable asking for what I want.

____Never   ____Sometimes   ____Always

I share my opinions with ease.

____Never   ____Sometimes   ____Always

I consider my audience's views before asking for something.

____Never   ____Sometimes   ____Always

I identify persuasive appeals before making a pitch.

____Never   ____Sometimes   ____Always

I use quantitative data or forecasts to support my ideas.

____Never   ____Sometimes   ____Always

When someone disagrees with me, I work collaboratively to find a solution.

____Never   ____Sometimes   ____Always

If you answered Never or Sometimes to even one of these questions, I invite you to continue reading and to be prepared to power up your influence.

7

ℐNCREASE YOUR ℐNFLUENCE

Blessed is the influence of one true, loving human soul on another.

~ George Eliot

- ▲ Don't ask, don't tell (not)
- ▲ AIM before you shoot
- ▲ Get down and dirty with data
- ▲ Keep up with the Joneses
- ▲ Get your foot in the door
- ▲ Offer the last pair in your size
- ▲ Develop a third story

When I ask you to imagine someone "influential," who is the first person that comes to mind? Close your eyes. Think a moment. When you've put a name to the question, open your eyes again, and read on.

What is most interesting here is not whom you chose, but whom you didn't. I'll take a wager that it wasn't your own name that came to mind. When we think of influence, we tend to think of people who have influence over us or people who depend on the power of persuasion for their livelihoods. We think of salespeople, fundraisers, and politicians. We often think of males.

At the foundation of influence is the quality of our tribe, something we discussed in the previous chapter. It is whom you know, and it is also how well you know them. Establishing credibility and enhancing your likability are the building blocks of influential power.

But if we're going to grow our influence, we must conquer our fear of selling. Why *selling*, you might ask? Because even if we're not selling a product or service, we're selling ourselves, or an idea, concept, or strategy that is important to us.

The truth is that most women, myself included, have at some point in their careers uttered a version of one of these negative phrases: *I'm really bad at sales. I'm not worth a darn at self-promotion. I'm not good at marketing.*

True, selling can be intimidating. And it is most intimidating when we don't know our audiences or when we feel like we're going in cold. Selling gets a lot easier if we do one thing: listen. We can only sell solutions with upsides if we take the time to understand our audiences, their points of pain, and their needs.

If you're questioning your selling skills, then I urge you to revisit Chapter 3, Listen Like a Leader. When you listen effectively, you gain the understanding and knowledge you'll need to influence direction and decision. To conquer my own fear of selling, I developed a pre-sales mantra: *This is going to be easy, because all I have to do is listen.* It's a magical mantra when it comes to closing the deal.

The ability to get an affirmative answer to what you want – whether it's support, funding, increased responsibility, a bump in pay, or a promotion – is influence. By definition, influence is the capacity to achieve, to affect, to shape, and to change. Its deal-sealing partner, persuasion, is what causes people to say: *Yes, I agree ... yes, I will ... yes, I do.*

A brief aside: The power of persuasion can, and often has been, used for evil intent. Not in this book. Our focus is on the development of a positive tool that will assist us in meeting our own personal needs, benefit our work, and help make this world even a wee bit better.

How do you personally measure your persuasive power over other people? None? Some? A great deal? I'll answer that for you. You certainly do have persuasive power over people, and probably more than you know. But if you're not hearing that sweet word *yes* as often as you'd like, it's time to power up your influence.

DON'T ASK, DON'T TELL (NOT)

The first and most crucial step in increasing your influence is to ask for what it is you want. It almost sounds too simple to be true, doesn't it? In your quest for a plum assignment or a promotion, recognize that there will always be a time when the answer is *no*. When is that time? When you don't ask.

The truth is that women tend to lack confidence when it comes to *asking*. In their book, *Women Don't Ask*, authors Linda Babcock and Sara Laschever assert that men are four times as likely to ask for a salary increase than women with the same qualifications. Moreover, by failing to negotiate a starting salary for her first job, a woman may end up sacrificing over half a million dollars in earnings over the course of her career. In other words, this tendency not to ask is akin to flushing dollars down the toilet.

Women are notorious for waiting. We wait for opportunity to knock instead of going out and creating it. We sit around waiting for others to make the magic and hope we get swept up in the process. Whether the request is as small as some assistance with childcare or as monumental as asking the person we love to marry us, you and I are less likely than a man in the exact same situation to ask.

I am obliged to note that a recent study from the non-profit group, Catalyst, suggests that women may indeed finally be asking for raises and promotions just as often as men do, but they're still less successful at getting them. I have not yet witnessed this trend personally, however. Let's explore a case-in-point involving Nora, an actual client of mine.

Nora was the Global Head of Operations at a Fortune 100 company and a very influential executive. She did such a fabulous job transforming her own division that her superiors invited her to take on a new role with even greater scope in a different division.

Nora wanted this new position badly. She even went so far as to outline an entire strategy for transforming this second division *before* her new title and responsibilities had been made public. And then, shortly before the announcement, she confessed to me that she had not yet discussed the new position's salary with her seniors and was scared to have the conversation. While few things surprise me at this point in my career, I admit I was a bit shocked that this powerful and capable woman was waiting for someone else to initiate the conversation.

Nora was jeopardizing her bargaining position by agreeing to assume increased responsibility without first negotiating her salary. She certainly did not want her position to be announced publicly before she clarified her compensation, so we moved into action. We found the language she would need to assert her position regarding salary, benefits, and perks, and role-played the conversation. Nora made an appointment that same day with the people who mattered, had a flawless conversation with them and, lo and behold, got exactly what she asked for.

Nora praised me endlessly for my help – attributing far more to me than was actually warranted. Then, a week or so later, when she asked to extend our coaching engagement, I fell into the very trap that she had.

I was excited to hear that she wanted to continue working together while she transitioned into her new role, and I said without thinking, "My rate has actually gone up since we contracted for your initial coaching engagement, but I'll just invoice you at the old rate."

Nora gave me an amused look and said rather matter-of-factly, "Why would you do that?!"

Frankly, I was ashamed. I was an Executive Coach with nearly two decades of experience under my belt, and I had succumbed to exactly the same thing she had. Nora's question was valid. Why *would* I do that? All I had to do was ask her to respect my new rates, and that would have sealed the deal. It was just a matter of asking for what I wanted.

There are many reasons why Nora and I, like so many other women, have trouble asking, and why women historically have not been very successful at asserting themselves. We've been taught that nice girls don't ask. We tend to focus more on the needs of others than our own. We fear being perceived as pushy. We like to be liked. We hate confrontation. The list goes on.

Unfortunately, this historical handicap doesn't end here. Not only do we not ask, we also don't tell. Telling, in this discussion, means asserting our perspective.

According to the OpEd Project, an organization that monitors the gender breakdown of contributors to "public thought-leadership forums," only 15% of participants are female. This figure also holds true for members of Congress and for writers on the *New York Times* editorial pages. Even Wikipedia, which hardly demands a high level of expertise, lists women contributors in the minority.

While I'm the first to acknowledge that our society needs to become more accepting of women asking and telling and that companies have to fix an inherent gender bias, these are not excuses to fall back on. If you have professional dreams – and it is unlikely that you would be reading this book if you didn't – then you have to push yourself to ask more and tell more.

Asking for what you want and telling what you know are necessary steps to gaining influence. And remember, being influential doesn't just mean getting the pay you deserve. It means opening the door to opportunities you desire, being a champion of meaningful ideas and groundbreaking strategies, shaping outcomes, and bringing good things to the people around you. All in all, it means managing your professional ascent to places where your skills and talents are maximized and where you will thrive and prosper.

It's time to reverse the female "Don't Ask, Don't Tell Policy," and the good news is, it's not that tough! Even better, I'm going to show you how.

Let's begin your breakthrough by identifying what it is that you want in the workplace. Here are some examples I've heard from my own clients:

I'd like to have more responsibility for logistics.
I'd like to be included in more senior meetings.
I want to move into a position with global responsibility.
I want to do less number crunching and more strategic planning.

To that end, fill in the blanks below.

1. I want _____
    _____.

2. I'd like to _____
    _____.

3. I want to do more of _____
    _____.

4. I want to do less of _____
    _____.

5. I want to work with _____
    _____.

6. I want to be part of _____
    _____.

Now read what you wrote aloud. How does it feel? There is something inspiring about seeing your needs spelled out and hearing them roll off your tongue.

AIM BEFORE YOU SHOOT

Now that you know what you want, it's time to figure out how to get it. A passionate desire is not sufficient, nor is a brilliant pitch. In fact, a pitch is only successful if you get exactly what you want from your audience.

Before you start planning your pitch, AIM strategically. By AIM, I mean focus on your **A**udience, your **I**ntent, and your **M**essage.

A	AUDIENCE
I	INTENT
M	MESSAGE

AUDIENCE

The A in AIM is for the Audience you're targeting.

- ▲ Who are they?
- ▲ What do they know about you?
- ▲ What do they know about your request?
- ▲ How will they respond?

Are you asking your boss, your boss's boss, or your peer? What are their perceptions of you and your work? Do they understand why you want what you want? What's their bias? What are their likely objections?

Answering these basic questions about your audience will make you an Olympics qualifier when it comes to accurate targeting.

INTENT

The I in AIM identifies your Intent.

An intent is similar to an objective. You can solidify your intent by answering this all-important question I introduced in Chapter 1:

After you communicate, what do you want your audience to know, think, or do?

I use this question frequently in sessions with my executive clients when they're telling me about upcoming meetings where they want to be influential. I ask, "What's your objective for this meeting?"

Invariably, their initial response will focus on the "I" word and will sound something like this:

I want to discuss an opportunity I have to be involved in our company's Asia Project.

With this version of an objective, there's not much to prepare or think about. You're all set to run into your boss's office and blurt out your needs and desires. You're not thinking about your target. This is like shooting before you AIM. It's potentially dangerous, and almost certainly doomed. You are likely to miss your target, and things may even backfire on you.

At this point with my clients, I repeat the Intent question, with special emphasis on my client's audience:

After you communicate, what do you want your audience to know, think, or do?

In other words, if you're hoping to hear the word *yes*, this has to be less about you and more about your audience.

The Intent question forces you to make your audience the focus of your thoughts and, therefore, the subject of your objective:

My boss will sign off on my participation in the Asia Project.

Notice the difference. As soon as you focus your intent on your audience, it naturally leads to the most obvious of questions: *How am I going to get my boss to do that?* It moves you into a mindset of strategic preparation. Now you're AIMing before you shoot.

MESSAGE

The M in AIM is for Message.

Now that you've articulated your intent, you can start crafting a message meant to elicit an unequivocal *yes* from your audience.

The fastest way to get there is to address what is called WIIFM, or *What's In It For Me?* Despite what we might like to believe, most of us are rather egocentric. We have our own interests and needs, and we generally put them front and center. When someone approaches us with a request, a part of our brain begins to calculate the personal impact of that request.

Therefore, if you want to be a persuasive communicator, assist your audience in determining exactly how your request or idea can benefit them personally.

Use Bulls-Eye Benefits

To answer that omnipresent, egocentric question, *What's In It For Me?* it's important to learn to use what I call *bulls-eye benefits*. This method targets the heart of the WIIFM question. It speaks directly to what's important to an audience and how a request, idea, product, or service can and will serve their best interest.

Nothing demonstrates the concept of bulls-eye benefits better than media advertising:

De Beers: *A Diamond is Forever.*

Groupon: *Live your City for Less.*

Even the U.S. Army has perfected its WIIFM pitch when it offers potential recruits the chance to *Be All You Can Be.*

And one of my favorites is the FedEx bulls-eye benefit that hits the target dead center: *When it absolutely, positively has to be there overnight.*

To demonstrate this winning strategy, let's return to our example of a request to become involved in a company's Asia Project. The woman taking AIM in this case is a client of mine named Emily, an Asian American who is fluent in Japanese.

The Asia Project was, in fact, an exciting opportunity presented to her at a time when she was losing some enthusiasm for her work and needed something to re-energize her. Before she got too carried away, however, her boss would have to agree to her participation. This was the perfect occasion to AIM before shooting.

First, Emily evaluated her **Audience**, who, in this case, was her boss Aubrey. Here's what Emily knew: Aubrey valued her contribution to his team and her skill set. He valued her work ethic and the way she got things done. She made Aubrey look good. Aubrey was never shy about giving her more responsibilities, and she always performed admirably.

When Emily mentioned the Asia opportunity to Aubrey in passing, however, he saw it as something that would likely distract from her primary work and quickly dismissed it.

Spelling out her **Intent** was easy for Emily:

I want my boss to support my desire to spend 10% of my time on the Asia Project.

Now, it was time for Emily to craft the **Message**. She began with the WIIFM question:

What's in it for Aubrey?

In the beginning, she came up blank. It was easy enough to think of how it benefited her, but not so easy to figure out the bulls-eye benefits for Aubrey. So Emily went back to the drawing board. She re-analyzed her audience. What about the Asia Project might Aubrey value?

For one, Aubrey was big on his team's contribution to the company's broader mission of comprehensive customer satisfaction on a global level. Emily knew that Asia was fast becoming a part of the company's expanding customer base, and if Aubrey understood how quickly this was happening, he might be more supportive of her participation in the Asia Project. Emily also knew how much pride Aubrey took in his reputation with his seniors. She realized she could also use this in answering her boss's WIIFM question, because the person who had first extended the Asia Project invitation to Emily was more senior than Aubrey and broadly respected in the company.

Emily now had two very solid bulls-eye benefits to use in her message to Aubrey:

1. She would be contributing to the company's mission to become more global.
2. Her inclusion in the Asia Project would catch the attention of the firm's most respected leaders, and Aubrey's reputation would benefit.

Head-Butt Objections

Sometimes, all you have to do is offer a bulls-eye benefit for your audience, and your dreams come true. More often than not, however, there are objections. But even in the face of the typical arguments – those relating to cost, risk, time, and effort – you will be most persuasive when you meet these potential objections head on.

4 COMMON OBJECTIONS

COST	It's too expensive!
RISK	It's too risky!
TIME	It will take too long!
EFFORT	It's too hard!

In Emily's case, she knew that her bulls-eye benefits weren't sufficiently persuasive and that there were big objections to counter. Aubrey's primary objection was that Emily's involvement in the Asia Project would detract from her primary responsibilities, and he couldn't afford to lose 10% of her focus and energy. With this in mind, she conceived a legitimate plan to replace 10% of her current workload with this new opportunity. By taking a leave from a leadership position on the firm's Community Service Committee and by delaying her involvement with the Mentoring Program, she added more clout to the message she would deliver to her boss, namely that her primary workload would be unaffected. She was ready to take full AIM.

You can use this same strategy to get what you want by identifying possible objections to your ideas, requests, or strategies in advance and head-butting them with compelling propositions. The following pages outline several persuasive appeals that are proven winners.

GET DOWN AND DIRTY WITH DATA

Often in business, it's the bottom line that speaks the loudest. The ultimate financial outcome calls the shots. This tells us that we have to support our ideas, requests, and strategies with quantitative data or forecasts that are credible, reliable, and understandable.

Now, before you have a chance to proclaim your math-phobia, I'm going to head-butt your objection by saying that this has nothing to do with math. Rather, this has to do with *financial storytelling*.

Financial storytelling is the art of using numbers to tell a story. We women are often masters at weaving captivating stories, so all we have to do is add bits and pieces of credible data to give them bottom-line punch.

If your tendency is to keep your distance from data, now is the time for you to strive to overcome it. In fact, when your success is riding on your ability to influence, getting your hands dirty with data is an absolute must.

You'll find that people are willing to support an idea when the benefits outweigh the costs. In order to present that argument, you must tell a persuasive bottom-line story that answers five fundamental questions with solid data:

1. **What do we lose by doing nothing?**
   Your audience may be comfortable with the status quo, therefore you must address the downside of doing nothing.

2. **What's the price tag?**
   Solving problems often costs money. Don't forget to include initial costs as well as those that might creep up in the future. Make sure your analysis is realistic.

3. **What do we gain?**
   Your audience will always be interested in the quantitative upside, in particular when it comes to revenue. But even while you're addressing the money side of things, don't forget the intangibles, like strengthening your client's perception of you or making the work process less complex.

4. **What do we save?**
   You always want to address how what you're proposing can save both money and time.

5. **When do we spend and when do we gain?**
   If your request is time-sensitive – and most are – your audience will want to know when it has to shell out and when it can expect a return.

In sum, you can become more expert in the quantitative arena and increase your workplace influence by adopting the following practices:

- ▲ Consider numbers to be your persuasive friends.
- ▲ Develop a comfort level with numerical analysis.
- ▲ Tap into the data experts or training resources around you.
- ▲ Identify a partner or mentor who can help you get down and dirty with data.

KEEP UP WITH THE JONESES

Although business people love to analyze problems logically or objectively, decision-making often has an emotional component. (If you don't believe me, just follow the wild fluctuations of the stock market for a week.) Therefore, your arsenal of persuasive appeals must have emotional impact.

Companies use *benchmarking* to measure themselves against competitors. But benchmarking is really just another way of "keeping up with the Joneses," and you can counter any number of objections to your request by citing what the other guys are doing and what you need to do to keep up.

We often take cues on how to behave from those around us, and business is no exception. If following the lead of other successful departments or companies can prevent mistakes or help further a cause, then make absolutely sure that your audience knows who else is doing what you're proposing. If you're asking for a bump in salary, make sure you know what other people in similar situations are making. If you're pitching an idea, find out if there is anyone else doing something similar. If they are doing it with wild success, make sure your audience knows it.

Those Joneses, whoever they are, can be mighty influential.

GET YOUR FOOT IN THE DOOR

Sometimes, the scope of what you want is just too overwhelming for your audience, and the last thing you want to do is turn your audience off by asking for too much. (Can you imagine asking to double your salary?)

The foot-in-the-door approach pitches only a fraction of what you hope to later achieve. The idea is to get your audience to bite. Once they make a commitment to your cause, even a small or seemingly trivial one, they're very likely in for the long haul. If your audience makes a small commitment publicly, verbally or in writing, they're likely to stay true to their commitment in the future.

My high-school-aged son is a master at getting his foot in the door. He's at that stage in life when it's important that he be assigned the best teachers for any and all of his classes. Unfortunately, the school's computers randomly determine who gets which teacher. School policy further dictates that you get what you get. No arguments.

My son has faced this prospect several times and has his own way of challenging the system. First, he visits his preferred teacher before the term starts. He proposes the idea of transferring and waits for the predictable, "Sorry, it's against school policy." Then, he sticks his foot in the door.

"I understand that," he says. "But is it okay if I sit in on the first few days of the class, just in case someone drops out?"

"There's no law against that," is essentially what the teacher always says, honored that a student would feel so strongly about her class. "But I'm not making any promises."

I have a feeling my son also uses another very effective persuasive appeal with the teacher – flattery! And you know what they say about flattery: It goes a long way.

So what happens? The term starts. My son attends the first few classes, behaves himself, and participates with gusto. The teacher in question invariably bends the rules and allows him to stay the course. This is a perfect example of how when you want something big, it can be very effective to slip your way in one toe at a time.

Likewise, arranging pre-alignment meetings – the powwow before the game or the mini-meeting before the big meeting – is a beneficial foot-in-the-door tactic. My most influential clients engage in these with peers, seniors, and vendors, encouraging them to reach agreements on small pieces of the bigger requests to come.

Once not only your toe but also your foot is in the door, it will be a lot easier to call on other persuasive appeals to increase your influence even further.

OFFER THE LAST PAIR IN YOUR SIZE

I love boots. I really love black boots. I have a lot of black boots, partly because I love them. But another reason I have so many is that each pair I own was, coincidentally, "the last pair left in my size." I fall for this selling ploy every time.

Robert Cialdini, the author of one of my all-time favorite business books, *Influence: The Psychology of Persuasion*, calls this the Scarcity Principle. This principle reflects that when something is too common, we value it less. However, if we perceive something as the "last pair left," our whole mindset changes. We've all heard the pitch: *Buy now while supplies last!* And we've all fallen for it.

At online flash shopping bazaars like Ruelala.com, a digital clock counts down the number of hours, minutes, and seconds you have left to get the absolute best, most desirable deal of the day. This can certainly move you into action.

For our purposes, the "last pair in your size" appeal is a very effective device when you're asking for something from your audience. The minute you identify a limited window of opportunity – it could be something as simple as a seasonal price from a supplier or a deadline for a decision – you set out a lure that will be hard for your audience to resist.

DEVELOP A THIRD STORY

Sometimes people fundamentally disagree. If I take any two of you and put you in a room together for a while, I'll bet you'll have at least one disagreement. It's not uncommon for two people to have very different ideas about an approach or strategy, whether it is how to best load the dishwasher or maximize profit. This presents a challenge because it's hard to be powerfully persuasive when there is fundamental disagreement. It's difficult to get your *yes*!

What to do?

I'm sure you've heard the expression: "There are two sides to every story." Disagreements are sometimes so severe that, never mind *sides*, it seems there are two very different *stories*. At the end of the day, there can be only one story, and unfortunately, it's not always yours. The good news is that the one story doesn't have to be your challenger's story either. What I am referring to is a new version called the Third Story.

The Third Story is not about holding up a white flag or conceding. It's about moving from disagreement to agreement while still allowing you to have a powerful say in the ultimate conclusion. The key to an effective Third Story is to stop advocating for your point of view and start understanding why you and your audience see things so differently.

To discover the Third Story, you'll once again have to power up your listening, using skills you learned in Chapter 3:

- ▲ Ask to hear your audience's story.
- ▲ Ask questions.
- ▲ Paraphrase your understanding.
- ▲ Empathize, if emotions are high.
- ▲ Tell your story.
- ▲ Generate a Third Story collaboratively.

The result? A win-win situation.

To make this come alive, let's consider Helmina, a client of mine, who is a Senior Vice-President of Technology. Recently, there was a high-profile project in the works at her firm, and Helmina was chomping at the bit for her Technology division to take the lead on it. However, the Engagement division in the company was also angling for the lead.

Helmina's task was to advocate with her seniors in favor of her division, so we began working on articulating persuasive appeals toward that end. Knowing that her seniors were always concerned with being first to market, Helmina used supporting data to argue the fact that her Technology group already had the needed funding and the technological expertise to launch the project quickly. She also employed the "Keeping up with Joneses" appeal by benchmarking the recent success of a competing firm using technological prowess in a parallel project.

Her seniors, however, weren't seeing it quite the same way. The SVP of the Engagement division had some powerful appeals of his own. His group, in particular, had social media know-how, which was absolutely necessary for the project's long-term success.

Instead of pushing until the relationships with her seniors and her peers were damaged, Helmina moved into the Third Story approach. In this version, Helmina's Technology group took the lead during the early phase of the project when speed was essential and then handed over the project to the Engagement group, so it could ensure long-term success with focus on community engagement and brand building via social media. Everyone bought in, and the new project was launched successfully.

When that *yes* is not coming easily or when there's rising conflict, remember that seniors or peers who might have different stories or agendas from yours are not workplace enemies. Incorporating the Third Story into your arsenal of persuasive appeals will allow you to transform opposing forces into collaborators or influential allies.

INFLUENCE WITH IMPACT

One last, yet important, reminder: It's not just *what* you ask and tell, but *how* you ask and tell. I encourage you to revisit the Communicate with Oomph skills from Chapter 1 – in particular the CAR and PREP formulas – as well as the Strut your Stuff skills from Chapter 2, as a means of increasing your influence even further.

Now get to work asking, telling, and growing your influence, and get ready to hear that sweet word – *yes!*

THE ELEVATOR WORKOUT

INCREASE YOUR INFLUENCE

I commit to power up my influence by:

_____ Asking for what I want

_____ Getting more comfortable with data

_____ AIMing more strategically with persuasive appeals

_____ Collaboratively developing a third story

To increase my influence, I will:

Stop: _____

_____

_____

_____

Start: _____

_____

_____

_____

Continue: _____

_____

_____

_____

POWER PROFILE

$\mathcal{K}$IM $\mathcal{G}$OODMAN

President
Global Business Travel
American Express

How does a woman who grew up in a working-class neighborhood on Chicago's south side find herself on *Fortune* magazine's list of the most powerful African-American executives in America? Meet Kim Goodman, the President of Global Business Travel at American Express, and the executive responsible for supporting 140 global markets. During her tenure at American Express, she's steered multibillion-dollar businesses and led over ten thousand employees to service more than three million customers.

Kim is also married with twins plus another little one, so as she herself puts it, she's "delightfully busy."

Needless to say, Kim wasn't exposed to the corporate world at an early age. Her mother was a teacher; her father serviced vending machines. She learned the value of an education and developed an unsurpassed work ethic. She earned degrees at Stanford and Harvard Business School and started her career with the consulting firm of Bain and Company. Consulting had its advantages. It exposed Kim to multifarious businesses, affording her valuable perspective on what worked and what didn't in corporate America. More than anything, it taught her the art of building relationships. But what Kim discovered is that there is a big difference between being an advisor and being a leader, and that is accountability. She wanted to be in the trenches, and she got her chance when she joined Dell Computer Corp, working for Michael Dell as his Vice-President of Development.

At Dell, she mastered five jobs in seven years and started and ran a new product line that generated $100 million in revenue in less than a year and a half and is still going strong today. She worked with their Public Sector (Government & Education) marketing and sales business and led their software and peripherals division, with overall responsibility for product marketing, vendor management, and pricing.

In 2007, she joined American Express with an acute understanding that a service-oriented company like American Express must first create value and then provide return on value. Kim has her own unique approach to leadership. She says: "I care deeply about people. When I come to work, I'm the most real person I can be. I'm not for one second ashamed that I bring my heart to the job. We all want to do something special and extraordinary in this world, and the best way to do that is through people. The second way is through innovation."

Kim describes innovation as that which is meaningful, different, and valuable in the marketplace. She says, "The questions I always ask our customers are: What do you need? What can help make you more efficient? How can we help you thrive?'"

Kim doesn't believe in hiding out in her corner office. She engages her team at every level, even accompanying them to meet with customers. Part of her job is to bring insight into the role her company can play in elevating a customer's business. In her list of cardinal leadership rules is one that reads: You follow through on what you say you're going to do, and you do it every time.

"I lead even when the hills are the steepest, but first I make sure the hills we're climbing are the most important ones to the company," Kim says, before turning to the subject of managing up. "When you're managing up, the people that you work for place high value on people they can trust. You have to have deep appreciation for what your leaders are trying to accomplish, the extreme pressures they are under, and the decisions they have to make. To be trustworthy, you have to bring your people the right insight and the right information. You have to care about their success, their wins."

Kim is a big believer in sponsorship. Sponsors are those special people who help promote your career, who can give you that nudge to the next level. "You earn sponsorship by earning someone's trust, always being reliable and following through," Kim says. "If you put in raw, hard work to make your company successful, then you'll find sponsorship. Greatness is only partially talent; your greatness is largely your focus, practice, and dedication. And that's exactly what I look for in the women I sponsor."

Kim's message to women riding the glass elevator reflects her own secret to success. She says: "Develop authenticity in your relationships 360 degrees – with your boss, your peers, your team, and your customers."

Just as important: "Lead from your heart."

THE GROUND FLOOR QUIZ
FIND THE ME IN TEAM

I know what makes me unique.

____Never   ____Sometimes   ____Always

I comfortably communicate my achievements to others.

____Never   ____Sometimes   ____Always

I Google myself.

____Never   ____Sometimes   ____Always

I update my LinkedIn profile and headshot.

____Never   ____Sometimes   ____Always

I engage in professional activity online.

____Never   ____Sometimes   ____Always

I participate in industry events and conferences.

____Never   ____Sometimes   ____Always

If you answered Never or Sometimes to even one of these questions, I invite you to continue reading and to be prepared to power up your personal brand.

8

$\mathcal{F}$IND THE ME IN $\mathcal{T}$EAM

Be a first-rate version of yourself,
not a second-rate version of someone else.

~ Judy Garland

- ▲ Be real
- ▲ Stay different
- ▲ Be relevant
- ▲ Toot your own orchestra
- ▲ Amplify your brand
- ▲ Increase your visibility
- ▲ Exude

I recently attended a friend's 50th birthday party. At one point in the festivities, her husband stood up to toast her. A lovely gesture, you might think. That's what I anticipated, until I heard what he had to say. He praised her for being a "selfless" mother and wife. *Selfless?!* Was that supposed to be a compliment? It took every ounce of my self-control to resist cringing.

I fantasized posing two questions to the husband's captive audience. First: *Have you ever heard of a man lauded as "selfless"?* And next: *Who in the world wants to be hailed as "selfless"?*

We no longer need Freud to remind us of the importance of a healthy self, or ego, to meet life's challenges head on and to be happy. With no self, who are you? Moreover, if you are a nothing, or are merely here to serve the needs of others, you are not much of a role model for your children or anyone else you aim to inspire.

A stereotypically female characteristic, selflessness is also rarely associated with success, especially in the workplace. It's confidence – and even competitiveness – that we associate with professional achievement. So it's no surprise that men are often praised for being confident and competitive leaders. When a man toots his own horn, it's considered darn good PR. Yet, when a woman trumpets her own achievement, she is oft-times scolded for not being a team player.

Here's the conundrum: If both selflessness and braggadocio are ill-advised, how exactly do we get noticed in the workplace? My answer is: Find the ME in Team.

It's time to discover what makes you personally shine and to share it with others. If you do it the right way, it will prove beneficial for you, for the people you work with, and even for your company.

The good news is that it's a perfect time to stand out in the workplace. Conformity is out; creativity is in. Companies that are innovative are the ones that succeed even in difficult economic times. These are the very same companies that are seeking out creative, innovative, and original professionals, the firms that value team members who stand up and stand out. They are the very organizations that want their employees to be influential and to leave their mark.

As marketing guru Seth Godin claims, "The only way to get what you're worth is to stand out, to exert emotional labor, to be seen as indispensable."

What does this mean for women in the workplace? It means that companies are welcoming more ME in Team. So let me help you find it.

BE REAL

You may know the term "personal branding," which has become a trendy phrase in the business lexicon. Many people don't connect with the word "brand," a term traditionally used for manufactured products. A personal brand may sound artificial to you. On the other hand, I don't think any of us would have trouble associating with the word "reputation." We all have a reputation of one sort or another. In fact, we all recognize the truth in the phrase, "Your reputation precedes you."

I'd like to suggest that your brand is like your reputation – you have one whether you like it or not. For better or worse, we are all brands. The aim is to have a brand in demand.

People choose strong brands, and we all desire to be chosen. We want to be selected by our seniors for meaningful tasks at work. We yearn for clients to embrace our ideas and services. We long to be singled out for recognition and appreciation. We want to be favored for promotion.

Your personal brand will help you realize these prospects. But first, understand that a personal brand is not something you hire a marketing team to dream up for you. A personal brand is authentic. It's real. It's that thing that makes you irreplaceable and different from everyone else.

If you're defined simply by a job title, you're not unique; you're replaceable. For instance, every doctor in this country has a medical degree. It's necessary; it's not an element that differentiates or distinguishes, nor is it the factor that causes you to give a referral to a friend. The reason you recommend your doctor is because of that something special that sets her apart. It could be her bedside manner and the way she listens; maybe it's the way she describes complex issues in layman (or "laywoman") terms. Perhaps she promotes preventative medicine or healthy lifestyle choices rather than being quick to prescribe drugs for every malady. Maybe she never keeps you waiting and returns your phone calls promptly. While a diploma is a "must-have," these other things you value are unique brand attributes.

Every job has a list of minimum "must-haves." What about yours? Must-haves are the types of requirements you often find on job descriptions, such as education, years of experience, and skill sets (like a working knowledge of Excel). In other words, they are proficiencies everyone needs to do your particular job – those everyone before you had, and the ones everyone after you will need.

To distinguish them from features that make you truly unique, take a minute to list the minimum must-haves for your current position.

What educational degree, if any, is required to do my job?

_____

What kind of experience, if any, is necessary for this role?

_____

_____

_____

_____

What skills are needed to do my job?

_____

_____

_____

This baseline list of job requirements will help you unearth what makes you unique in the workplace.

STAY DIFFERENT

Clearly, more than one person has the minimum must-haves to do your job, but each person would do the work differently. It's the special touch you bring to the job that distinguishes you from the pack. You are not fitting into a mold, but creating one that is distinctively your own.

No two brands are the same. When we take a look at the world of big brands, we know that Kmart and Target are both in the business of selling household products at relatively cheap prices. From there, however, their brands diverge. Kmart has a no-frills approach. Target, on the other hand, has a chic, fun way of merchandising. I remember my niece being such a fan of Target as a child that her grandparents regularly bought her Target gift cards for her birthday. Can you imagine a girl getting excited about a gift card from Kmart?

It's time to unearth the brand attributes that make you stand out. What makes *you* special? What makes *you* unique? These may be tough questions for some of you, because women, generally speaking, have not been raised to toot their own horns. These questions will help you extract the ME from Team:

What words do people use to describe me at work?

_____

_____

_____

What descriptive words consistently appear on my performance reviews?

_____

_____

_____

What types of tasks or work projects am I often selected for?

_____

_____

_____

What am I known for at work?

_____

_____

_____

Keeping in mind that the most successful women leaders are self-aware, be brave and ask members of your family, a couple of your friends, and two or three of your co-workers some similar questions:

What three adjectives would you use to describe me?

_____

_____

What tasks or projects do you always think of me for?

_____

_____

When you take time to reflect and seek input from others, a picture of your most desirable strengths will emerge. This is an illustration of what differentiates you at work.

As you ride up the glass elevator, moving from one position to another, your list of must-haves will change and expand. Yet, your special touch – your very own personal brand – will remain intact.

BE RELEVANT

You have to be real and you have to stand out, but you also have to be relevant to your workplace audience. To be chosen, you have to offer something needed. To be cherished, you have to add value.

Being relevant doesn't mean being all things to all people. You're working way too hard if you're trying that approach. It's far easier to be known at work for one or two things that make you shine and set you apart.

You know this is true from the products you consciously and unconsciously choose every day. Imagine this: You're a mother shopping for a car to chauffer your kids around in, and the feature that is most important to you is safety. Hmmm … cars and safety … what's the first car that comes to mind? I bet it's *Volvo*. While a Volvo shares many excellent characteristics with other cars, it is best known for a single trait. People who value safety above all other car attributes are very likely to check out a Volvo before making a purchase. In other words, safety is the most relevant benefit to Volvo's target audience. If you're shopping for say, a Ferrari, however, other features probably come to mind. Though a Ferrari may well be a safe vehicle, safety is not likely to be the number one item on your list of criteria.

Like product brands, people with strong personal brands have one feature that stands out. Take Oprah. Now there's a brand if ever there was one. What is Oprah most known for? She cares. She's built her entire lucrative empire around her caring brand.

Think for a moment. What special feature do you consistently bring to the table at work? Of all the wonderful qualities you listed on the previous page, which is most compelling and most valued by your boss, your seniors, your HR leaders, your co-workers, and your industry contacts? If you're still having trouble answering this, be patient and kind to yourself, and simply answer:

Which of my many brand characteristics would I like to be known for?

_____

_____

_____

Contemplating being known for something singular and wonderful might feel a bit out of character for some of you. But as Oscar Wilde put it: "The only thing worse than being talked about is not being talked about."

TOOT YOUR OWN ORCHESTRA

Every successful executive I know emphasizes the necessity of not only doing stellar work but also of tooting her own horn. I know each of you is dedicated to doing great work. I also know that many women are not completely comfortable with the notion of calling attention to their achievements.

Reframing self-promotion as a means of sharing what you can contribute is helpful. But to ease you further into the notion of self-promotion as critical to your professional ascent, I suggest you start by "tooting your own orchestra," the players being your team or the people you've partnered with on projects. Tooting your own orchestra involves directing a spotlight on their triumphs. When you talk about their success, your own leadership skills are apparent. And as you celebrate the achievements of your peers, your collaborative ability shines through. This is good prep for tooting your own horn. Nudge yourself in that direction by occasionally dropping an "I" (instead of the royal "we" that female team players prefer) into the praise you heap on others. In other words, talk about how you contributed to the team's success or what role you personally played in facilitating a productive working environment. Here's how it might sound:

The team completely embraced this project and ran with it. I'm thrilled with their success, and also gratified that the time I spent drafting the strategy and divvying up responsibilities paid off.

While you gave the team the bulk of the credit in the above scenario, you also made it clear – without hogging the spotlight – who pulled the strings.

We talked in Chapter 7 about the power of reciprocation, and when you toot your own orchestra, you create reciprocal opportunity. In simple terms, trumpeting a colleague's achievement will very likely cause her to trumpet yours.

You might say, for example:

Shanna was the perfect partner on this project. Her warmth and personal attention to every person on the client team definitely influenced them to go with our proposal.

When you point out a colleague's unique brand attribute in this way, it will naturally encourage her to highlight yours in return. And there is another payoff to be gained: your peers and seniors will notice your positive attitude and your motivational style. In tooting your own orchestra, you unwittingly and powerfully augment your own desirable brand.

AMPLIFY YOUR BRAND

Once you find the ME in Team, it's time to point it out to others in your company. When the powers-that-be become aware of you as a valuable resource, you will become more influential. Let me also remind you that many men around you are unabashedly tooting their own horns and often with the amp on high volume. You don't have to play by their rules, but you must be assertive about how you can contribute to the cause and positively influence the outcome.

One of my favorite questions for my clients is: *Who needs to know?* In other words, who needs to know about your skills, your achievements, and your aspirations? Start by making a list of your target market inside your company. That's right: every brand has a target market. Even you. Make a checklist, starting with the internal people on the list of your twelve to eighteen core tribe members you formulated in Chapter 6. Is there anyone you want to add to the list? Consider seniors, peers, and contacts from other departments, such as Human Resources and Public Relations.

Your aim is to keep your internal target market up to date on all things *you* – how you're growing professionally, the special projects you've taken on, and your significant contributions. Make a plan to connect regularly with all the people on this list and to consciously amplify your brand.

INCREASE YOUR VISIBILITY

Riding the glass elevator up the ranks of any organization has a distinct advantage: the view expands. You begin to see things within the scope of your organization you never noticed from the levels below. You see the bigger picture, in terms of people, product, and process, with greater acuity. As you're doing so, ask yourself: *How visible am I to others?*

One test of your external visibility is the strength of your online identity. After all, what's the first thing we all do to check someone out? We Google them! It is therefore vital to assess whether you are digitally distinct or digitally disastrous. There's a great way to find out. Google yourself and then take the quiz offered by Reach at:

　⌐ http://onlineidcalculator.com

The calculator helps make sense of your Google results and provides insight about the online visibility of your growing brand.

COMMUNICATE ONLINE

The more active you are in social media, the more professionally visible you are. Even if you choose not to participate actively in social media platforms like Twitter, at minimum you have to be visible to professional connections through a well-managed LinkedIn profile. Please tell me you have one. And please tell me you've included a headshot (and not one of your baby or dog!). If not, it's time to get to work. Go to http://LinkedIn.com and get started.

If you already have a profile, check to see if it is a generic portrayal of the "must-haves" of your job or an active reflection of your unique brand. With that in mind, take a look at these two LinkedIn profiles for career coaches:

Shall Remain Nameless, Career Coach
Career Development Professional who specializes in Career Coaching, Training and Development, and Outplacement Career Counseling

Susan Whitcomb, Career Coach
I grew up painfully shy. As a 'farm-town' kid (hometown Firebaugh, California, then population of less than 2,000), I know how hard it can be to find your voice ... to live with confidence ... to believe there will be "enough" of the things you need to succeed. Career coaching opened the door for me to find that voice, to live with confidence, and succeed with significance. And I'm on a mission to help others accomplish the same.

Need I say more? Remarkably, but perhaps not so surprisingly, exactly one week after Susan Whitcomb replaced a traditional, stiff LinkedIn bio with the one you just read, she got an email from a columnist from *Fortune* magazine who was intrigued by her bio and wanted to interview her for an article. Bottom line: Authenticity works.

Authenticity in your online profile and written bio means moving away from a job description and telling a more dynamic story. Talk about yourself, the ME in Team, in an original voice.

And as I mentioned, don't underestimate the need for a headshot. People want to connect a name with a face. Professionals are more likely to read something you've written if you appear real to them. First impressions last, so make sure you use a high-quality photo that exudes your personal brand. Notice the glowing photos in the power profiles of this book.

As you build your online presence and increase your visibility beyond the confines of your company, revisit the question: *Who needs to know?* Consider your external constituency, such as customers, vendors, and industry peers. Every time you participate online, you automatically become more visible to your broader tribe.

Commit yourself to adding something new to your online activity on a regular basis. Here are several ideas to spur you on:

- ▲ Comment on a career-related forum.
- ▲ Post items of interest.
- ▲ Blog or guest-blog.
- ▲ Write an article for an industry magazine.
- ▲ Co-write an article with a client for an industry site.
- ▲ Write a career-related book review.

Make it a goal to communicate regularly with your target audience. Pick something that you love to do. I personally have a "vlog," a video-blog. I communicate with my target market by blasting out monthly two-minute videos with tips for professional success. If you'd like to receive them too, subscribe to my vlog on my website:

⌐🖰   http://oracoaching.com

When people compliment me on my brand "marketing," I am always momentarily surprised. It's so much fun to make these videos that it never feels like a marketing chore. And my target market loves them to boot. So whatever online activity you choose, make sure you enjoy it. Your enthusiasm will be contagious.

COMMUNICATE FACE TO FACE

You increase your value at work when you establish Leadership Presence in the external marketplace, not only online but also "offline." By offline, I mean parting with your technology and communicating "in the flesh." When you promote yourself expertly in person, you enhance your company's image as well. And naturally, if the going ever gets rough, having a broad network of industry contacts who have witnessed the way you stand out can land you back on your feet quickly.

There are many ways to amplify your brand in person. Here are some ideas to help you actively introduce your expertise to the broader professional community:

- Ⓐ Volunteer at an industry event.
- Ⓐ Assume a leadership position in a professional organization.
- Ⓐ Speak at an industry meeting or conference.
- Ⓐ Host an internal meeting on trends of interest.
- Ⓐ Arrange a roundtable for industry guests.

When you share your energy in person, you leave an indelible shadow of your powerful presence.

EXUDE

Once you've found the ME in Team, it's time to exude it with clarity, consistency, and constancy. Every time you *engage* and *connect*, you have the opportunity to communicate not only what you do, but also how you do it uniquely.

When you *strut your stuff*, your personal style communicates your brand visually. When you *communicate with oomph* and *listen like a leader*, your credibility and expertise shine through. Every interaction, whether you're *tangoing with your team* or *buddying up with your boss*, is an opportunity to demonstrate your value. When you *grow your tribe*, you extend the reach of your professional contribution.

As William Arruda, personal branding guru and my best advisor, likes to say, "To be outstanding, stand out." And when you stand out, you'll gain the power to influence the world in the way that you choose.

THE ELEVATOR WORKOUT

FIND THE ME IN TEAM

I commit to power up my personal brand by:

_____ Sharing my contributions more actively

_____ Updating my bio and headshot

_____ Participating in an online professional activity

_____ Becoming involved in an industry organization

To find the me in team, I will:

Stop: _____

_____

_____

_____

Start: _____

_____

_____

_____

Continue: _____

_____

_____

_____

POWER PROFILE

*M*ICHELLE *G*LOECKLER

Senior Vice-President
Walmart, GMM Home Division

You may have heard the sentiment: "Everything I know as a C-level executive, I learned as a waitress."

No, Michelle Gloeckler didn't use those exact words, but she did say, "I was a really good waitress." It was during her years in the restaurant business that she learned to make order out of chaos. "I had the ability to organize a sequence of food orders in my head and could take far more tables than the other waiters. I knew instinctively how to group orders, hot and cold, and when to serve them for maximum efficiency. It was also important to give the customers the service they wanted. Were they in a hurry? Did they want to chat and joke? Were they conducting business?"

Michelle was only sixteen at the time, but she'd made a personal discovery. "Everyone has a gem to offer at every level. You have to figure out what that gem is and share it."

Michelle's numerous gems have propelled her to her current position as the Senior Vice-President of Walmart's Home Division, where she oversees buying, branding, and product development for the company's Cook & Dine, Bed & Bath, Décor, Home Organization, and Outdoor Living categories.

Before her ascent at Walmart, Michelle followed her mom – a sales rep with Wrigley – into the food business. She went to work for The Hershey Company right after graduating from the University of Michigan and spent 21 very successful years with the company.

"Mom gave me the confidence that I could raise a family and be successful at work at the same time," Michelle says. "The key to being successful in the workplace is to understand what you're good at and then put yourself in a role that uses those strengths. Women in particular are afraid to talk about their strengths and we have to get over that. It's okay to let folks know. You instill confidence when you say, 'I'm good at that. Let me take that on.'"

Michelle wore many different hats at Hershey and was willing to relocate any number of times to support her career, spending time in Hershey, Charlotte, Raleigh, New York, Texas, and Detroit. At Walmart, she has been equally flexible, staying open to the many roles that came her way.

"Sometimes the most successful career moves you make are the ones you don't plan," she says. At Walmart, it was the company's CEO who suggested she move into the Home Division when she thought she was more suited for a similar position in Grocery.

"The element of surprise can be your ally," she says. "I went into something I hadn't planned on and ended up loving it. That is not to say that you're going to love every aspect of your job. Some parts can be a drag. But you have to be tenacious. You have to look at every situation as a learning opportunity."

No matter how big or complicated the project, Michelle always reminds herself that creating order out of chaos is one of her strengths. "I know it's okay when I don't have all the answers, because as a leader, you have to depend on your team."

In addition to her ability to multi-task, Michelle lists three essential tools in her ongoing professional success: people leadership, financial management, and resilience.

"A people leader," she explains, "is a good listener. You have to be able to take ideas from the people around you and create an environment where diverse thought is not only welcome but celebrated. I look at myself as a facilitator. I like to get the best out of people."

On the other hand, Michelle is quick to recognize not only her strengths but also her weaknesses. "I like to make things happen and move on. But sometimes I move too quickly. I have to tell myself to slow down and get the best thinking from all stakeholders. I can deliver better results if I include more thoughts and input from people around me."

Volunteering is also something that Michelle believes in strongly. She is currently the Chairman of the Board of NEW (see http://newonline.org), a not-for-profit dedicated to the advancement and retention of women in the retail and consumer goods industry. "Getting involved and helping people has been great for my professional career. I encourage women to volunteer for something they're passionate about and something where they're going to gain experience that their job doesn't offer."

Michelle is also a wife and mother, and she insists that a successful career and a happy family are a natural match. "You can do both, and you can do both well … as long as you remember to pick up the pizza."

THE GROUND FLOOR QUIZ
BE HAPPY

I feel in control of my schedule.

____Never   ____Sometimes   ____Always

I eat foods that energize me.

____Never   ____Sometimes   ____Always

I have an exercise routine.

____Never   ____Sometimes   ____Always

I get enough sleep.

____Never   ____Sometimes   ____Always

I pursue hobbies and activities that make me happy.

____Never   ____Sometimes   ____Always

I seek new challenges and opportunities at work.

____Never   ____Sometimes   ____Always

If you answered Never or Sometimes to even one of these questions, I invite you to continue reading and to be prepared to power up your happiness.

9

$\mathcal{B}$E $\mathcal{H}$APPY

Be happy. It's one way of being wise.

~ Colette

- ▲ Reduce the overwhelm
- ▲ Be an energy factory
- ▲ Bring back the joy
- ▲ Take the plunge
- ▲ Say the magic words

Happiness is the new holy grail. Everyone's talking about it. Everybody's searching for it.

In the last few years, books with the word *happy* in the title have been crowding bookstore shelves. An Internet search for the word *happy* yields nearly three billion results. Harvard Business School even offers a course on happiness, and students are flocking to it.

So how does this search for the 21st-century holy grail fit into the workplace? To begin with, a growing number of women claim that their jobs are a necessary ingredient in their quest for happiness. I feel the same way about my work. As it turns out – and perhaps not so surprisingly – the converse is true as well: Happiness is a necessary ingredient in our professional achievement.

Happy leaders make more productive leaders. In fact, in a sweeping meta-analysis of 225 academic studies reported in *Harvard Business Review*, researchers found that happy employees have, on average, 31%

higher productivity. Their sales are also 37% greater, and their creativity is three times higher.

The exploding field of neuroscience is one of the many reasons happiness has become such a hot topic. Without getting too technical, it's worth noting that it's now possible to track brain physiology with sophisticated magnetic resonance imaging technology. What this means is that scientists can pinpoint the exact location in the brain associated with certain functions, like the smile.

When we smile, experts can tell us exactly which part of the brain responds to the stimulus. Why is this important? Because we have long been fascinated with whether we could influence the happiness center of the brain, and that possibility has now become a reality. It turns out that we have more control over happiness physiology than was thought even a decade ago.

Apparently your grandmother was right when she would say: "Take that frown off your face and put a smile on. You'll feel better!" Maybe it was woman's intuition or just years of experience at work, but Grandma knew her stuff.

Even more fascinating is the result of another recent scientific study, proving that when your facial muscles are manipulated into a smile using a machine, your happiness center responds with an unmistakable glow. Even when you force a smile – which we all do on occasion – you spark the joy center in the brain. Soon you're no longer forcing that smile – your true feeling of happiness causes it to happen naturally.

To explore this intriguing topic further, let's examine insight from one of the most compelling research books written on the subject, *The How of Happiness*. In it, author Sonja Lyubomirsky summarizes the three factors that play a significant part in determining our inner joy.

The first, and most dominant, are the genetically determined set points we were born with, which contribute 50% to our happiness level, an indication that some people are simply predestined to be happier.

A meager 10% of our happiness is directly related to life circumstances, such as economics and health, meaning you're likely to be happier the more financially secure and healthier you are, but just slightly.

This leaves a whopping 40% of our happiness in our own hands, revealing that our ability to control what we do, with whom we associate, and how we think can significantly influence our happiness quotient. This unexpected level of control makes us mighty powerful, if only we choose to exert it.

HAPPINESS FACTORS

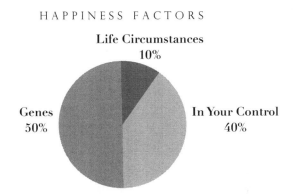

Let's think about this in work terms. In the best of circumstances, we would all feel on top of the world in the workplace – happy to get up on Monday mornings, energized with our significant and meaningful work, engaged with the people at the office. When things don't feel exactly this way, our natural instinct is to blame the work, attack the people, or criticize the company.

But not so fast. Instead of baring your teeth, let's make sure you're boosting your happiness through the kinds of personal choices that are fully in your control. After all, happy leaders are the ones we find influencing corporate direction and charging up the organizational chart.

REDUCE THE OVERWHELM

We women shoulder countless diverse responsibilities, and we're pretty darn good at it. We are multi-talented multi-taskers. Most of us have to-do lists that are out of control and self-perpetuating; what we don't add to the lists ourselves, we allow others to add. But overall, we get things done, and we do them well.

These facts likely indicate that your brain, like mine, is in overload a good deal of the time. Do you sometimes ask yourself: *How can I possibly get it all done?* Do you sometimes lose track of everything that needs to be accomplished? For many women, the answer is *yes*. And if you're like many others, there are occasions when your growing to-do list makes you more or less miserable and probably not a lot of fun to be around.

If only we all had the rather amazing mental capacities of Professor Albus Dumbledore, the headmaster in J.K. Rowling's *Harry Potter* series. He possesses an enviable ability to siphon off information from his brain, organize it in separate vials, and then access each bundle of information from a "pensieve" when needed. Now that's a skill worth having.

But fantasy solution aside, what we've come to unequivocally understand is this: To feel happy, we need to feel in control. In order to do that, we have to reduce what I call "the overwhelm," which involves kicking in some time-management strategies. And while we can't organize our to-dos into vials like the ineffable Professor Dumbledore, I can certainly help you to manage them better.

Introducing the four Ds of time management:

- ▲ Delete
- ▲ Delegate
- ▲ Do, but Diminish
- ▲ Delay

These four actions will not only reduce the overwhelm, but they will effectively open up time and space for you to attend to the things that are most important in your life – the things that make you happy. They are, therefore, strategies worth mastering.

DELETE

Believe it or not, there are some things on our to-do lists that we simply don't have to do. Take a look at your own list. I'll bet there are at least one or two things you can cross off right now. For example, do you really have to visit four potential summer camps, or can you accept credible testimony from other parents?

You get the idea. Prioritize your list and delete where possible. You'll be surprised how good it feels. Yes, I recognize that this can be easier said than done, given how invested most of us are in our personal to-do lists. But if you look at it purely from a timesaving perspective, deleting becomes less painful and pays dividends almost immediately.

DELEGATE

If you want to do bigger and better things, like tackle a challenge at work, you're going to have to stop doing some of the smaller, less important things on your list. In short: You need to lighten the load and sharpen your focus.

If someone else *can* do it or *should* do it, then it's time to delegate. True, you'll have to learn to let go, something some women struggle with. There is always the risk that the delegate might not perform the task with the same level of perfection, enthusiasm, or flair as you might. But does it make a big difference? If the answer is *no*, then let that person carry it out. If it does matter, then find someone who can do the job as well, if not better, than you can, or someone who can learn to do it.

To ease your way into delegating, my advice is to start with your home responsibilities, if your life involves living with family. Your partner is capable of doing the dishes or pushing a broom. Your children can run the vacuum cleaner or tidy up their rooms.

When my three kids were little, doing the laundry was my most time-consuming, never-ending job in the house. The piles never seemed to get smaller despite the constant rumble of the washing machine. One day, I went cold turkey. I gathered my husband and children and summarily announced that they would henceforth be responsible for their own laundry. So what if my littlest one had to stand on a chair to reach the dryer? It was an easy machine to run. With a single act of parental and spousal delegation, I was liberated. My kids, as it turned out, were proud of their newfound responsibilities and didn't require a lot of nagging. I'm also blessed with a husband who naturally assumes 50% of the chores.

Think about it. What did I have to let go of other than my aversion to the occasional unfolded piles of laundry in my kids' bedrooms and my obsession with perfectly straightened drawers? In exchange for these minor pet peeves, I not only freed up my time, but also taught my kids a lesson about responsibility.

As a woman running my own business, I don't have a full-time staff working for me, but I've still learned to delegate small work tasks that take precious time away from my first priority: coaching senior executives. Coaching is what energizes me and makes me happy. I hire professionals for all the rest: legal, accounting, clerical, and technology. The expense is well worth it. In fact, the more I delegate, the more my career grows. The same will be true for you.

There is also a silver lining to this delegation business. When you delegate in the workplace, you give the gift of growth. Actually, you give a double gift of growth. First, you give your delegates a sense of ownership, which is a major motivating force. You also show your trust in their abilities and provide them with an opportunity to grow. Second, you give yourself the time, space, and energy that power *you* up for professional growth.

DO, BUT DIMINISH

Yes, I know. There are some things you *must* do and others that *only* you can do. Beyond that, there are things you *want* to do because they make you happy. In all of these cases, there may be an abbreviated method you can utilize to ease the load.

Let's take an example from the personal side of things: the school bake sale. You want to help out and allow your child to see you participating. And maybe you feel the homey urge to bake brownies instead of buying them. The Do, but Diminish formula says you can still *do* the task, but in a *diminished* way. Solution? Pull out the speedy Betty Crocker mix instead of baking from scratch.

This same formula applies to the workplace. Let's say you're a leader who likes to acknowledge your employees' birthdays with individual celebrations. A wonderful gesture, but since a party for every employee can be a time drain, consider giving a handwritten note or card on the actual date and reserving the party for a monthly group gathering. This way, each employee receives your personalized wishes and has the fun of a celebration, while you've allotted yourself more time for other responsibilities.

While attention to detail is of significant value in the workplace, not all tasks demand the same level of thoroughness. Precisely because some of us women have a tendency to overdo in many areas, ask yourself if there is a diminished way to do any one task at hand without sacrificing achievement.

DELAY

Contrary to how you may feel, not everything needs to be done today. In fact, some things may not need to be done this week, this month, or even this year. When your to-do list is growing a bit too quickly, take a closer look at it. The decision to delay a task or two will likely allow you to concentrate on the most critical things. Deliberately postponing a task that isn't a priority is also an immediate mood booster. Try it and see.

BE AN ENERGY FACTORY

When you delete, delegate, diminish, or delay, you naturally free up some energy.

But to do heavy lifting in the workplace (and I'm not talking about rearranging the furniture), you need a constant supply of vim and vigor. Do you have enough right now to be productive, creative, and happy both at home and at work? If you're hesitating, you're going to have to become, as I like to put it, an energy factory.

Almost too obvious to name, but often taken for granted, there are three fundamentals of energy production: food, exercise, and sleep.

While we women tend to be obsessed with our bodies and eating habits, we can all probably admit to overlooking at least one of these three on a regular basis. Thus, we are neglecting an opportunity to maximize our energy.

I have encouraging news for you: By tweaking just a few habits in your life, you can boost your vivacity, become happier, and ultimately increase the stamina you require for upward propulsion.

GET REAL WITH FOOD

It only takes one trip to your local bookstore to realize that diet books are as popular as ever, so a discussion of food should grab our attention. We women seem to have an insatiable appetite for information about the latest and greatest diets, despite the fact that most diets don't work, at least not over the long haul.

So my advice on the subject is simple. Forget dieting; focus instead on increasing your energy, and your diet will take care of itself. Zero in on foods that energize you, and your weight and fitness will respond accordingly. I guarantee it.

Here's my secret to having the vibrancy you will need to take on more responsibility in the workplace: 80% of the food you eat should look like "real food." Real food comes from a natural source, such as a tree, the soil, or the ocean, and you can pretty much rely on it to give you energy. A simple way to follow this advice is to ask yourself before eating: *Does this food resemble nature?* For example: cotton candy doesn't; carrots do. Donuts don't; dates do. Fries don't; fish does. Not too hard, huh? And if 80% of your food looks like real food, you won't have to sweat the other 20%.

GET OFF YOUR BUM

Let's face it: Exercise is hard for some people. For others, like me, it's harder *not* to exercise. I'm so reliant on the happy chemicals released in my brain when I exercise that I feel downright yucky (to use a technical term) if I don't. Exercise is the third thing I do every morning, and to keep it motivating, I mix it up. One day I'll run; the next I'll lift weights. I also bike, box, and do yoga.

"I don't have time to exercise" is the most common rationalization people use to explain this missing component in their lives. (I counter this by reminding them that the busiest, most successful executives I know exercise regularly.) But the truth is, exercise energizes you. It allows you to do more, and it releases hormones that naturally make you happier. So to achieve this more blissful state, I encourage you to ... yes ... get off your bum.

Research clearly shows that you don't need to be an Ironman (or "Ironwoman") triathlete to reap the energizing benefits of exercise. Simply get moving. Park your car at the far end of the lot to get in extra steps. Take the stairs. Walk with a colleague at lunch. Ask a loved one to stroll with you in the evening.

One client of mine arranged a Walking Club at work. The members meet at 8:30 a.m. in their suits and sneakers and briskly walk every floor in their building, just to get the juices flowing. And they note the added benefit of greeting everyone as they arrive in the morning and interacting, if only briefly, with colleagues they might not otherwise see during the day. By 9:00, they're at their desks and ready to take on the day.

That bum booster works for them. Now all you have to do is find out what works for you.

SLEEP YOUR WAY TO THE TOP

Literally. Get your *ZZZs*. This should be a no-brainer. Study after study proves without doubt that people function best after seven or eight hours of sleep. Although our own bodies and minds are the best barometer when it comes to this, it's no surprise that sleep deprivation can adversely affect your concentration and your memory. In fact, in a recent study of pilots on long flights, non-napping pilots experienced a 34% *decrease* in reaction rate over the course of the flight. Conversely, when pilots napped for just thirty minutes, they experienced a 16% *increase* in their reaction rates.

But wait, it gets even better. Studies also demonstrate that people who sleep more have better immune function and live longer. Beyond that, those same people are more attractive and less likely to get fat. (Yes, there *is* such a thing as beauty sleep!) What more evidence should a woman need to inspire a good night's rest?

Still not convinced? Well, there's more. A good night's sleep definitively improves your productivity, both at work and at home. And best of all, the more you sleep, the better your mood!

Bottom line: Sleep makes you happier.

With all of this positive data, however, the sad truth is that women these days are sleeping only an average of six hours a night, so all the benefits we just described go right out the door.

If you're one of those six-hours-a-night-or-less gals, then I encourage you to start focusing on that extra hour or so of much-needed sleep. If you find that difficult to do, here are a few tips to get you started:

- Delegate tasks.
- Cut down on alcohol and caffeine.
- Know when to call it a day.
- Commit to a time to turn out the lights.
- Create a wind-down ritual that works for you.

And finally, if you find your mind bombarded with thoughts come the witching hour, take a page out of Dumbledore's book and siphon the distractions or worries out. If there are no magic vials around into which you can deposit your intrusive thoughts, simply write them down.

After all, tomorrow is another day, and getting adequate rest will enable you to wake feeling happy and energized for family, work, and play.

ASK THE FOUR QUESTIONS

For the majority of the population, daylight hours are for working and playing, for being productive and creative, and for growing and changing; nighttime hours are for sleeping. So whenever I find my energy lagging or my eyes closing in the middle of the day, I get concerned. Not freaked-out concerned, but enough to ask myself my four personal energy management questions:

1. *Did I get enough sleep?*
2. *Am I over-caffeinated? ***
3. *Did I eat too much white sugar or white flour?*
4. *Did I drink enough water?*

* This may sound counterintuitive, but if you're depending on caffeine for energy, you're bound to crash when it wears off.

These are questions that don't take a lot of probing, but the answers take me directly to the root of my energy imbalance. Then I work on tweaking my habits so that I regain the vitality I need to be the best I can be with my clients and, of course, with my family.

What are your four energy questions?

Spend a couple of minutes thinking about the things that drag you down, realizing that your questions may be different from mine. Yours might involve a lack of exercise or too much nighttime activity, too much television at bedtime or a missed meal during the day. Whatever you come up with, write them down.

My four personal energy management questions:

1. _____
_____.

2. _____
_____.

3. _____
_____.

4. _____
_____.

Put your list next to your computer, on your bathroom mirror, in your purse, or in your i-device. Then, when the droop hits, don't kick yourself – just survey your four questions. Answer truthfully and make the necessary changes to your routine. Each tweak will boost your energy and make you happier.

BRING BACK THE JOY

As we mature, we naturally start attending to the needs of others and get busier with things like chauffeuring our kids or caring for our parents. By sheer mathematics, this means that we're attending less to ourselves. We become more concerned with the happiness of others and forget many of the things that used to nourish our souls and evoke those moments of unfettered joy.

Has it been a while since you curled up in bed with a juicy book? Is your knitting project languishing in the closet? Has a chunk of time passed since you volunteered for a cause close to your heart?

An important question to ask yourself is:

What activity did I love to do in the past that I am no longer doing?

For me, the answer was dancing, so I decided to put that cherished activity back into my routine.

If there's something that's slipped from *your* life, find a way to reintroduce it. Each of us derives joy and happiness from different activities and avocations. Indulge yourself, even if it's with small tastes of something that brings you joy. The result will be that extra burst of happy energy that will help propel you toward success in all areas of your life.

TAKE THE PLUNGE

Once you're feeling energized and joyful, it's time to do something new, challenging, exhilarating, and even scary. Why? Because feeling a bit uncomfortable and getting over it is a great way to grow.

If you're a bean counter and don't take risks, you'll always be a bean counter. If you have dreams, forsaking risk will leave you professionally stuck. But let's face it – taking risks doesn't come easily to most people. We often fear potential consequences, including failure. As Shakespeare eloquently wrote in *Measure for Measure*: "Our doubts are traitors, and make us lose the good we oft might win, by fearing to attempt." He reminds us that if we're afraid to try, we sacrifice opportunity.

Eleanor Roosevelt – first lady, author, speaker, politician, and advocate for civil rights – once said: "You must do the things you think you cannot do." You may be surprised to learn that despite all of her accomplishments, Eleanor Roosevelt was far from fearless. In fact, she was proud to admit that she was compelled every day to do something that scared her. She pushed beyond her comfort level, and the result was the evolution of one of our most admired and accomplished Americans.

Much like Eleanor Roosevelt, almost every executive I interviewed for this book used the words, "I took a risk." In your professional pursuits, I encourage you to do the same.

If you're not inclined to do so already, start by trying something new and different. I suggest you explore something in your personal life as a parallel growth experiment to your workplace adventure. Because of my affinity for physical challenges, I forced myself to try pole dancing, which was out of my comfort zone. I'm the kind of person who freaks out if my feet are not on the ground, so for me, hanging upside down and depending entirely on the strength of my thighs was frightening. The first time I tried the move, my heart was beating so hard and my body was shaking so ferociously that I lasted little more than a second. But I stuck with it, and over time it became fun. I discovered how graceful I could be, even hanging upside down. And now I'm proud of myself for going out on a limb (literally!). I pushed past the discomfort, and ended up upside down and happy.

You can apply this same concept to trying something new and challenging at work; the rules are no different. Accepting assignments that are challenging and unexpected, even if the thought of them scares the pants off you, can ultimately fill you with a huge sense of accomplishment. Jumping at new career opportunities can be risky as well, but risk is always a road worth traveling when your dream position is on an upper floor.

Companies value professionals who welcome challenge. Leaders hold in high regard professional women who are willing to take on new responsibilities, who are open to testing the waters of the new and different, and who are well rounded.

To be one of those women, stay open. Make a list of things you'd like to try, and keep your eyes peeled for any opportunity to participate in special projects and task forces. When an opportunity comes your way, ask yourself, *What's the downside?* Then, use these tips:

- ▲ Weigh the obstacles of starting something new against what you'll gain from mastering it.
- ▲ Balance what you could learn against what could go wrong.
- ▲ Remind yourself that mistakes are terrific learning opportunities.
- ▲ Remember that failure is just another reason to press ahead.
- ▲ Line up the resources and support you'll need to succeed.

Once you've shifted your mindset, take the plunge. Offer your time and talent, despite your apprehensions. When you take risks, you're stimulated. And when you're stimulated, you grow professionally. And that makes us women downright happy.

SAY THE MAGIC WORDS

No matter our age, a simple *thank you* is more powerful than we know. In fact, research has shown that a practice of gratitude can boost our moods and make us measurably happier. Now that's what I call a practice worth its weight in gold.

Psychological research has gone even further, proving that positive emotions are associated with higher levels of creativity, increased problem-solving ability, and greater overall success in life.

Outward gestures and expressions of thanks are positive, meaningful, and simply good manners. But inner gratitude is equally important. A practice of gratitude means bringing more conscious appreciation into our lives by establishing habits or rituals that engrain thankfulness into our being. There are many ways to do this. Prayer works for some people. Keeping a gratitude journal works for others. Singling out one person each day and sharing a simple "Thanks for being in my life" can go a long way. I know people who incorporate *thank yous* into their family dinner ritual.

Whatever your mode of expression, devoting yourself to a daily articulation of gratitude is healthy and empowering. I experimented with the idea of a regular, pre-bedtime moment of thanks, but it didn't work – I was way too sleepy. I've had better luck incorporating a moment of gratitude into my stroll back home after my morning exercise routine. Yes, the better my workout and the more beautiful the day, the easier it is to be thankful. But even if my body is aching and the sky is overcast, I try to find some little thing to be grateful for – it could even be the simplicity of hot coffee waiting for me at home. Ultimately, the important takeaway is the *ritual* of gratitude rather than the *object* of it.

On our upward ascent in the glass elevator, what would you guess is the most important thing we should be grateful for? I'll tell you what I believe the answer is: Ourselves. Contrary to what we may have been taught as girls, it's healthy to be thankful for who we are as individuals and what we have to offer the world. Allow yourself to find moments to be grateful for your work, to mark your economic achievement, and to celebrate your professional success.

I promise that saying "thank you" on a daily basis will make you happy. And I guarantee you that happy people outperform unhappy people every day of the week.

Be one of them.

THE ELEVATOR WORKOUT

BE HAPPY

I commit to power up my happiness by:

_____ Managing my time
_____ Maximizing my energy
_____ Engaging in joyful activities
_____ Taking risks
_____ Practicing gratitude

To be happy, I will:

Stop: _____
_____
_____
_____

Start: _____
_____
_____
_____

Continue: _____
_____
_____
_____

POWER PROFILE

 ONIKA  ANTILLA

President/CEO
Altura Capital Group

Monika Mantilla is one of the most powerful, well-respected Latina businesswomen in the country, and she has a refreshing philosophy: "While work and building companies is what I do, family is my source of strength, growth, and joy. I also love to learn new things, meet interesting people, dance, and laugh. These are the essentials." Hard to go wrong with this approach to life.

Monika is the founder of Altura Capital Group, a company that oversees the management of more than S6 billion in assets and serves more than twelve of the largest institutional investors in the world. "Our firm was founded in 2005," she says, "with one and only one vision in mind: To provide institutional investors access to the best source of emerging-manager talent in the country and the world."

What Altura does is provide institutional investors with customized manager-to-manager investment solutions. If an investor has a special need, Altura finds the firm for the job. Their investment advisory and research services cover more than 1,800 emerging and diverse managers in the business.

Monika's unique approach has earned her recognition as one of the Most Influential Leaders in Hispanic USA. She also received the highest honor for Latinos by Latinos when she was awarded the Hispanic Heritage Award in the business category.

This powerful leader's path to her current station as CEO, wife, and mother of two daughters began in Bogotá, Colombia, where she was born and raised. In describing her decision to come to the United States, she says: "It was love that brought me to the US. My husband was beginning his career in New York, so we decided to move and start our family here."

Monika was seventeen when she graduated from high school and twenty-two when she received her law degree with top honors. She joined a Latin-American multinational corporation and was promoted nine times in nine years. In her last position as Managing Director for North America, her responsibilities included financial management, a field to which she felt strongly attracted. Her firm then sponsored her enrollment at Columbia Business School, where she pursued her curiosity about the financial world and discovered her true niche.

In retrospect, while Monika may have chosen to study business early in her educational path, she also realizes the value of her law degree. "It gave me the ability to think critically, organize ideas, and develop an intellectual framework, skills that are very useful for finance and business administration." She adds: "Some things we choose and others are given to us, but the important thing is that we decide what to do with what we have."

Monika believes that all people and all communities, minorities or otherwise, can be the architects of their own success. "Success," she says, "takes persistence and perseverance. Persistence means you keep knocking on doors. Perseverance means you bring a thoughtful comprehensive approach for the moment. And, of course, obstacles are just things to resolve."

Her formula for success includes an almost obsessive commitment to time management. "Managing your time is a way to execute vision," she says, "so start by putting vision into your calendar."

Monika does this with her 90-10 rule. For 90% of her calendar events, Monika makes absolutely certain that she can articulate the objective before attending. The other 10% is left open for life surprises, "which are always valuable."

Her advice for women wanting to ride the glass elevator to the top is straightforward: "Know that your capacity is huge. It is bigger than you know. Work hard. If your boss asks for three things, give her six instead. I know that if you strive to cultivate yourself, grow, and work hard, you will find joy."

$\mathcal{A}$ FTERWORD

When I was in the 4th grade, I sent my Grandma Flora a story I wrote. She sent it back with a typed note (as you might remember from my Introduction, she was a fabulous typist):

Some day you will write a book.

I never forgot her message. Yet, it took me about forty years to start writing a book. Why? Because it seemed like a monumental project. It was too hard, too time-consuming, too overwhelming. It was something only other people could do, not me.

Writing this book turned out to be none of the above. Frankly, I found it entirely doable, and not because I have superior brain capacity or off-the-charts intellect. I certainly don't. I'm just an Executive Coach who is incredibly passionate about helping professionals enhance their Leadership Presence.

How, then, did writing a book transform from a daunting notion to a pleasurable reality?

I realized that if I could write an email, I could write a blog, and if I could write a blog, I could write a chapter, and if I could write a chapter, I could write many chapters. And if I could write many chapters, I could …. Well, you get the picture.

As they say in the writing business, "One page at a time." My point is that any ambitious goal is simply a bunch of baby steps put together.

Growing my tribe and tapping into its strength also made writing a book less intimidating. I am truly grateful for the help I received. I have many thank yous. To William Arruda, for coaching me to believe in myself. To Roman Milisec, for emotional inspiration. To Mark Graham, for punch. To Stacey Aaronson, for perfection delivered with unflagging cheer. To Noa Bendit-Shtull and Simcha Shtull for their wickedly wise eyes. To family, friends, and colleagues for support. And to 85 Broads for its commitment to provide a glass elevator for every professional woman. Yes, it truly takes a village to do just about anything these days.

There is just one thing you must do yourself. You must start the journey by taking the first step. I can promise you that the Glass Elevator will go up. How do I know? Because I've witnessed countless professional women taking the very same ride to the top that you envision for yourself.

What I can't guarantee is a consistently smooth ride. There will certainly be times when you get that sinking feeling in your stomach. You might experience the urge to exit before you've reached your floor. At those times, I hope you will come back to this book. Reading it anew and from a different point on your journey, I know you will discover insights to renew your faith in yourself and reinvigorate your effort.

Every now and then you might even find yourself stuck, unsure which way to go or quite what to do next. Remember you are not alone. The people you cherish and trust are alongside you.

Give yourself the gifts of patience and perseverance. Take it one elevator workout at a time.

When you take that first step into the Glass Elevator, you will immediately power up your Leadership Presence. Go ahead. Be engaging: Communicate with oomph. Strut your stuff. Listen like a leader. Connect deeply and broadly: Buddy up with your boss. Tango with your team. Grow your tribe. Be persuasive: Increase your influence. Find the ME in team. Be happy.

I know you will soar.

P.S. I want to continue to support you on your professional ascent, so I will add new videos with tips for success to my website regularly. Subscribe to my vlog on my site or connect with me to receive updates.

http://www.oracoaching.com
http://www.facebook.com/ORA.Executive.Coach
http://www.linkedin.com/in/orashtull
http://twitter.com/coachora

$\mathcal{A}$BOUT $\mathcal{O}$RA

Ora Shtull is an Executive Coach at leading companies in New York City, where she helps senior leaders power up their Leadership Presence. Executives who have worked with Ora over the past 15 years are thriving at their jobs, being promoted, and making seamless transitions.

In addition to coaching high potential NY executives, Ora has served as Adjunct Professor of Business Communication at NYU Stern School of Business. She is a featured speaker at conferences across the US, inspiring leaders to communicate with confidence and lead with impact. Ora was also a winner in the 2011 British Airways Face of Opportunity Contest, allowing her to begin extending the impact of her coaching globally.

Ora's undergraduate degree is from the University of Pennsylvania and her MBA is from Columbia Business School. She is certified as an Executive Coach by iCoach NY and has advanced training in Shadow Coaching, Fierce Conversations, Difficult Conversations, Crucial Conversations, MBTI, Clark Wilson 360, Leadership Agility 360, Julie Morgenstern Time Management, and Reach Personal Branding.

Ora feels blessed to live in New York City with her husband and three children. She stays energized by running, boxing, and practicing yoga.

85Broads

www.85broads.com

85 Broads is a global women's network whose mission is to generate exceptional professional and social value for its members. Through their regional network events and online at 85Broads.com, members invest their time, their intellect, and their financial capital in each other's ideas and businesses.

85 Broads was founded in 1997 as a network for current and former Goldman Sachs women who worked at **85 Broad Street**, the firm's NYC headquarters, and at other GS offices worldwide. In 2000, at the urging of women at Harvard Business School, they expanded the network to include women who were students and alumnae of the world's leading graduate business schools, irrespective of chosen career path.

In 2004, they recognized the importance of further expanding the network to include women at the undergraduate level who were pursuing every career path imaginable. Over the next three years, they created campus clubs at 40 colleges in the US and abroad.

And in 2007, they extended membership in 85 Broads to **all amazing, trailblazing women worldwide** without regard to one's college or graduate school affiliation.

The women in 85 Broads are entrepreneurs, investment bankers, consultants, filmmakers, bloggers, lawyers, educators, athletes, venture capitalists, portfolio managers, political leaders, philanthropists, doctors, engineers, artists, scientists, and all women who are seeking to blaze exciting new trails.

MEMBERSHIP BENEFITS

Online services: Access to the profiles and email addresses of 30,000 members worldwide through the Advanced Member Search, company SPOTLIGHT pages, Job Board, Events Calendar, Blogs, Videos from past events, Jam Sessions on hot topics, and a variety of social media tools.

Offline services: Exclusive regional chapter events and on-campus events at member colleges and universities.

85 BROADS CHAPTERS

Regional Chapters develop and strengthen a global presence through exclusive workshops and events featuring industry and career experts. New chapters are created at members' request and are organized and run by members of the network who passionately believe in the value of investing in, and learning from, smart women – from student to senior executive – globally. 85 Broads has active chapters in 35 cities around the world.

CAMPUS PRESENCE

85 Broads has student members at hundreds of undergraduate and graduate schools worldwide. Campus clubs host conferences on topics of interest including wealth management, career development, and ways to live your most empowered life! They also provide a forum for undergraduate and graduate school members to develop and hone their leadership skills, which dramatically increases their lifetime "return" on their education.

85 BROADS PUBLISHING

In 2011, 85 Broads began collaborating with brilliant members of their network who were authoring new books. Given their deep distribution channel, 85 Broads was the ideal partner to market books written by their members globally. 85 Broads is delighted to publish and promote the works of all great authors within their network!

LEARN MORE ABOUT 85 BROADS:

Information: www.85broads.com/who_we_are
Application: www.85broads.com/welcome
Facebook: https://www.facebook.com/pages/85-Broads/25558491898
Twitter: @85broads
Email: info@85broads.com